COLLINS GEM

BIRDS

Jim Flegg

**Photographic Consultants
David and Jean Hosking**

HarperCollins*Publishers*

HarperCollins Publishers
PO Box, Glasgow G4 0NB

First published 1994
This edition published 1999

Reprint 10 9 8 7 6 5 4 3 2 1 0

The copyright in the photographs belongs to the following photographers from the Frank Lane Picture Agency:
H. D. Brandl 30, 84, 124, 175, 207, 221, 226; C. Brown 40, 155, 185, M. Callan 17, 19, 27, 97, 214, 251; B. B. Casals 189, 203; H. Clark 166, 168; W. S. Clark 58, 59; K. Delport 31; Eichhorn/Zingel 153; M. Gore 150, 188, 197, 237; A. R. Hamblin 23, 33, 54, 65, 75, 89, 105, 111, 112, 120, 128, 135, 163, 164, 171, 179, 182, 187, 200, 202, 215, 222, 232, 240; H. Hautala 73, 143; J. Hawkins 18, 62, 72, 78, 141, 152, 158, 160, 161, 170, 178, 194, 198, 210, 230, 234, 242, 243, 249, 250; P. Heard 32, 224; E. & D. Hosking 20, 25, 28, 29, 35, 46, 48, 51, 52, 61, 67, 69, 79, 83, 87, 88, 92, 104, 121, 127, 132, 134, 136, 137, 138, 139, 193, 195, 205, 206, 208, 223, 228, 235, 238, 239, 246, 248; D. Hosking 36, 53, 63, 86, 94, 103, 140, 212, 220; R. Hosking 37, 144; L. Hue 47; P. Moore 126; H. Newman 74; P. Perry 71, 117, 118, 142; F. Polking 22, 60, 68; A. J. Roberts 122; D. A. Robinson 133, 217; Silvestris 57, 64, 146, 191, 225; P. Surana 26; R. Tidman 34, 56, 77, 80, 95, 96, 98, 99, 102, 107, 108, 114, 123, 131, 151, 169, 183, 192, 236, 244; J. Tinning 45, 167; B. S. Turner 216; M. Walker 154, 213, 218; J. Watkins 119, 130, 177, 219; A. Wharton 43, 147, 156, 211, 245; R. Wilmshurst 38, 39, 41, 42, 44, 49, 50, 55, 76, 81, 82, 90, 93, 100, 101, 106, 113, 116, 125, 145, 148, 157, 159, 162, 165, 172, 173, 180, 181, 184, 186, 190, 196, 199, 201, 209, 229, 231, 233, 241, 252; W. Wisniewski 91, 110, 115, 149, 174, 247; M. B. Withers 23, 66, 70, 109, 129, 176, 204, 227.

ISBN 0 00 472262-0

Printed in Italy by Amadeus S.p.A.

CONTENTS KEY

The birds in this book fall into 27 broad family groupings, each of which is identified by a typical silhouette at the top of the page. Birds are highly mobile and versatile creatures, and occasionally their anatomical adaptations to a particular way of life may outweigh family similarities. For example, swallows and swifts, so similar in appearance, are unrelated, and cranes (which look like herons) are actually related to the crakes and rails. In such cases, for ease of use the page heading silhouette is that which makes identification easiest for the birdwatcher.

 Divers (*Gaviiformes*) (p. 17) and **Grebes** (*Podicipediformes*) (pp. 18-19) are specialist diving birds of both fresh and salt waters, hunting fish and other small aquatic animals. Divers are slim and short-necked, grebes plumper: both have feet with lobed toes set back near a stumpy tail. Their wings are small, beat rapidly, and they fly relatively infrequently.

 Fulmars (*Procellariiformes*) (p.20) are oceanic seabirds with beaks showing clear signs of segmentation and with conspicuous paired tubular nostrils on the ridge. They are masters of energy-efficient gliding, and come ashore only to breed. They feed on fish and plankton caught near the surface.

Gannets and Cormorants (*Pelecaniformes*) (pp. 21-23) are large fish-eating waterbirds, characterised by powerful beaks. Gannets are maritime, spend most time in the air and dive spectacularly; cormorants spend more time on the water (fresh or salt), dive from the surface, and pursue prey underwater propelled by their large feet with all four toes joined by webbing.

Herons and allies (*Ciconiiformes*) (pp. 24-31) and **Crane** (*Gruiformes*) (p.84) are notably long-legged, long-necked wetland birds feeding on various small animals. Most are large, some huge. They have long, dagger-like beaks and stab at their prey. Some have adapted to drier habitats.

 Swans, Geese and Ducks (*Anseriformes*) (pp. 32-56) form a uniform family, generally aquatic (fresh and salt waters), some carnivorous, others vegetarian. Many dabble for food, while others dive. All are characterised by 'duck-like' beaks and by their triangular webbed feet.

 Birds of Prey (*Accipitriformes* and *Falconiformes*) (pp. 57-72) are often called 'raptors', and are characterised by relatively large effective eyes, markedly hooked beaks for tearing flesh (all are carnivorous or scavengers) and by long, usually bare lower legs ending in sharply hooked talons. Females are often substantially larger than males.

 Game Birds (*Galliformes*) (pp. 73-80) and **Rails** (*Gruiformes*) (pp.81-83) are generally omnivorous and characterised by bulky bodies and comparatively small heads. Short rounded wings lift them rapidly into flight. Game birds are terrestrial, with upright stance, running powerfully. Rails are marshland birds, with long legs and large feet. Some swim well, some dive.

 Waders (*Charadriiformes*) (pp. 85-113) are shoreline or marshland birds, feeding on a variety of small invertebrate animals. Most are relatively long-legged, with long toes. Most important identification features to observe (beside plumage colour) are beak length and shape, wing and tail flight patterns and leg colour.

Skuas, Gulls and Terns (*Charadriiformes*) (pp. 114-127) are long-winged web-footed seabirds. Skuas are oceanic or coastal, piratical or predatory, but can fish for themselves. Gulls are more omnivorous, larger species predatory, ancestrally coastal but now often occur inland. Terns are smaller, slimmer, shorter-legged, with longer slimmer wings, and dive from the air for small fish prey. Gulls often, skuas and terns rarely, rest on the water.

Auks (*Charadriiformes*) (pp. 128-130) are robustly dumpy, short-necked seabirds with short narrow wings and whirring flight. They feed on fish caught by diving from the surface and pursue their prey underwater, propelled by their wings.

Pigeons (*Columbiformes*) (pp.131-134) are heavy-bodied, small-headed vegetarian (largely seed-eating) birds with fast direct flight. There is no distinction between pigeons and doves.

Cuckoo (*Cuculiformes*) (p.135) and **Nightjar** (*Caprimulgiformes*) (p.144) are long-tailed birds with short pointed wings. Both are short-legged and have small beaks, feeding on insects, which are caught in flight by nightjars.

Owls (*Strigiformes*) (pp. 136-143) are characteristically stocky, with short tails and an upright stance. Large heads and big eyes surrounded by a prominent facial disc indicate largely nocturnal life-styles. Small animal prey is captured in powerful sharp talons.

Kingfisher, Bee-eater, Roller, Hoopoe (*Coraciiformes*) (pp. 147-150) form a group with little in common anatomically, but all sufficiently brightly coloured to be readily identified. All are carnivorous, their prey ranging from insects to lizards and fish.

Woodpeckers (*Piciformes*) (pp. 151-155) form a close-knit group, featuring a strong straight dagger-like beak, long, strong central tail feathers used as a prop when perched on trunks, and powerful feet with toes distinctively arranged two pointing forward, two back. Their flight is undulating, their calls strident, their drumming far-carrying.

Larks, Pipits and Wagtails (*Passeriformes*: *Alaudidae, Motacillidae*) (pp. 156-165) are largely terrestrial, swift running birds of open habitats. Larks and pipits are heavily streaked and well camouflaged, with a long hind claw; wagtails are more colourful, with long incessantly wagged tails. All eat insects and small soil invertebrates, larks also eat vegetable matter.

Swallows and Martins (*Passeriformes*: *Hirundinidae*) (pp. 166-168) and **Swifts** (*Apodiformes*) (p. 145-146) have short legs, small beaks, streamlined bodies and slim curved wings. Much time is spent on the wing, including catching insect prey and drinking. Swallows and swifts are taxonomically unrelated, but evolution has shaped the outward anatomy of both groups to suit a common life style.

Wren, Dipper, Dunnock (*Passeriformes*: *Troglodytidae, Cinclidae, Prunellidae*) (pp. 170-172)—

a grouping of convenience, rather than indicating close relationship. All, though, are predominantly brown in plumage, largely terrestrial in habit, (the dipper aquatic) and feed on small invertebrate animals, the wren using a finely pointed beak, the others more robust. The sexes are broadly similar.

 Thrushes and Chats (*Passeriformes: Turdidae*) (pp. 173-188) form an obviously coherent grouping with two major types. Thrushes are larger, stouter-legged and rather longer-tailed, often with a horizontal body posture. Chats are smaller, rounder in the body, with longer, slimmer legs and characteristically flick wings and tail. All share a medium-length pointed beak, stronger in some than others, and have a mixed diet of invertebrate animals augmented by berries.

 Warblers and Crests (*Passeriformes: Sylviidae*) (pp. 189-208) also form a coherent grouping of small birds, mostly migrants, dividing into distinctive sub-groups, the tiny generally greenish, active canopy-feeding leaf warblers and crests; the brown, sometimes streaked, reedbed *Acrocephalus* warblers and their allies; and the more robust and colourful *Sylvia* warblers, where the sexes differ in plumage. All have shortish insectivorous beaks, and depend heavily on insect food, though turning readily to fruit to augment their diet in autumn.

 Flycatchers (*Passeriformes: Muscicapidae*) (pp. 209-210). Small, migrant, and rather warbler-like, flycatchers share the habit of catching insect prey in flight. They are short-legged, giving an elongated, horizontal perching posture. Their beaks though short and pointed are broad, with bristles round the gape to increase their catching area, and often close with an audible snap.

Tits and Allies (*Passeriformes: Paridae, Aegithalidae, Timaliidae*) (pp. 211-218). True tits are small, active and agile woodland birds with relatively strong legs and a stubby but powerful beak well suited to an omnivorous diet. They nest in holes which they may either excavate or modify. Long-tailed and bearded tits are not closely related, but possess tit-like beaks and agility. These build complex nests in vegetation.

Nuthatch and Treecreeper (*Passeriformes: Sittidae and Certhiidae*) (pp. 219-220). Short-legged and with strong feet, these spend much time clinging to trunks and branches. Nuthatches are woodpecker-like in beak and habits (but lack strong central tail feathers). Treecreepers have large eyes and longish, finely pointed beaks to extract insect prey from crevices in the bark.

Shrikes (*Passeriformes: Laniidae*) (pp. 222-223). A close-knit group of relatively long-tailed, thrush-sized birds, with falcon-like hooked and notched beaks for grasping and tearing small animal and insect prey, which they sometimes impale on thorns for later consumption. Usually favour exposed perches.

Crows (*Passeriformes: Corvidae*) (pp.224-231). Large among the Passeriformes, crows are usually gregarious in habit and omnivorous in diet. All have powerful beaks, and are opportunist predators as well as scavengers. The true crows are black or blackish, related genera are more strikingly coloured (eg magpies, jays).

Oriole, Starlings, Waxwing (*Passeriformes: Oriolidae, Sturnidae, Bombycillidae*) (pp. 221, 232, 169) are similar in size and shape, flying fast and straight on triangular wings. Short-medium length straight beaks suit a mixed diet of fruit and invertebrate animals. Plumage and calls are best distinctive features.

Sparrows, Buntings and Finches (*Passeriformes: Passeridae, Emberizidae, Fringillidae*) (pp. 233-252) are small, stocky, rather short-legged, predominantly seed-eating birds, often gregarious. Their beaks are stout and roughly wedge-shaped. Upper mandible ridge is convex in sparrows; lower mandible distinctively larger than upper in buntings. In finches the precise size and shape of the generally triangular beak is a guide to diet and often useful in identification.

INTRODUCTION

This book gives easily-used identification details linked to full colour photographs, plus information on habitat, food, song and behaviour, for over 230 European birds, covering the species that most birdwatchers could expect to see in a lifetime. This introduction provides advice on how birds use the various habitats in our countryside, on the equipment needed for birdwatching, and on how to get the best out of your birdwatching by developing all-important fieldcraft skills.

Parts of a bird

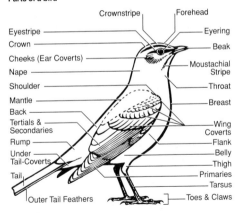

- Crownstripe
- Forehead
- Eyestripe
- Eyering
- Crown
- Beak
- Cheeks (Ear Coverts)
- Moustachial Stripe
- Nape
- Throat
- Shoulder
- Breast
- Mantle
- Back
- Wing Coverts
- Tertials & Secondaries
- Flank
- Rump
- Belly
- Under Tail-Coverts
- Thigh
- Tail
- Primaries
- Tarsus
- Outer Tail Feathers
- Toes & Claws

Habitats and migration

Unpredictability is very much a feature of bird life. The most distinctive character of birds (apart from their unique covering of feathers) is their ability to fly. Birds **migrate** to take advantage of opportunites in one part of the world which last only for part of the year — for example food being plentiful in one area in summer and another in winter. This explains the kaleidoscopic seasonal changes to be seen as migrants depart or arrive. Migration may be over huge distances, from the Arctic Circle to southern Africa or beyond, or be comparatively short-haul. Although this Gem guide covers the birds of the whole of Europe, many birds which do not breed or overwinter in your area will be seen as they come through on passage in spring and autumn. The ability to migrate (occasionally getting blown off course), coupled in many birds with an opportunistic approach to feeding, means that most birds do not necessarily conform to land boundaries laid down by geographers. Migration adds a great deal to the richness of birdwatching.

Nor do birds always stay neatly in the **habitat** categories that ecologists have attempted to draw for them. Although most of the ducks are associated with the sea or freshwater, kingfishers and dippers with rivers and streams, many birds are not so tidy. Kestrels may be seen over towns, coasts, moorland and motorway, and the gulls are as much at home on farmland and rubbish tip as at sea. Even Blue Tits, traditionally year-round woodland birds, may in midwinter be found in an oakwood, or (equally likely) feeding on an exotic food like peanuts in gardens (or opening milk bottles on town doorsteps to remove the cream), or feeding on insects hibernating in the shelter of the reed stems in a huge, tree-less marsh! In this guide, for each bird we identify the main habitats frequented.

Plumage

Even the **plumage** of birds changes with time. Feathers are the most obvious external feature of birds, and in many cases are brightly coloured and patterned. Though to us attractive, this patterning serves practical purposes such as attracting a mate, defending a territory, or helping with camouflage. For birdwatchers, plumage is often one of the best identification aids, but there are reasons for caution: as a general rule, males tend to be brighter, and females and immatures duller, as for them camouflage is more important than display. But in many species, the males in winter may also be drab, their bright colours only appearing as the feathers gradually wear down early in the spring.

In most birds, particularly the smaller ones, wear and tear during the year is balanced each autumn by the process called moult, when old feathers gradually fall out and are replaced by new ones. Young birds, two or three months out of the nest, lose their juvenile, often speckled plumage and grow the coloured feathers of the adult for the first time. As this happens, their plumage is a confusing patchwork of old and new. In larger birds like some gulls and birds of prey, the change from juvenile to adult plumage is gradual over three or four years, giving a series of immature plumages making identification quite a problem.

Birdwatching equipment

Perhaps the one essential piece of equipment is a pair of **binoculars**: with these, distant black dots take on an identifyable shape and colour, or the beautiful feather detail of a Great Tit feeding on a garden peanut-holder can be revealed. Binoculars range from cheap to expensive, so a choice over cost and which magnification you will need must be made. There are a few simple guidelines: the binoculars are for you, so they should be comfortable in the hand, easy to use and comfortable hanging round your neck — so do test them outdoors before purchasing. Optical quality tends to increase with price, so with cheaper binoculars (many of which are perfectly satisfactory), check that there are no colour fringes to the images you see, and that telephone poles are not 'bent' by poor lens design. If you wear spectacles, check that you can use the binoculars without removing (or scratching) them. As to magnification, generally avoid more than x10 as they are sensitive to shaking, and let in rather little light. For garden, field and woodland watching, x7 or x8 should be right, if possible with a 'wide angle' field of view. For those who birdwatch mostly on moorland, the coast, estuaries or large reservoirs, x10 is probably the ideal, although these binoculars will be heavier.

A **notebook** in which you can jot down notes of numbers of species and plumage details and make sketches (particularly of birds new to you) is also a necessity. Take notes immediately you see a new bird: these could turn frustration into satisfaction as the identification problem is later resolved. A pocket fieldguide such as this Gem should always be with you - in your pocket.

As to **clothing**, common sense is the best guide, but there are points to remember. Avoid bright colours and noisy rustling fabrics. Remember that in exposed habitats, the weather can change (usually for the worse) with surprising speed, so it is always worth having ample warm, wind and waterproof gear. A heavy sweater and a lightweight nylon kagoul or anorak covers most circumstances. On the feet, trainers or baseball boots may be adequate, but on rougher terrain, walking boots may be desirable, and wellingtons are obviously a necessity in wetland habitats. And always take a supply of energy-rich **food** and **drink** on longer walks.

Fieldcraft

In fieldcraft, the aim is to see birds well without being seen yourself. Experienced birdwatchers rely very much on their ears to give early warning of what is about. Knowlege of bird calls and songs is an invaluable aid to identification: experience is the best teacher, but listening to commercially available recordings is an excellent foundation. Birds also use their ears — the less chatter, laughter and cracking of twigs, the closer you will get. Pause often to **listen and look**, preferably in a sheltered spot with a good view. Try to merge into the background, using natural features like banks, hedges and sea walls to avoid standing above the skyline. On the coast or in estuaries, check the **tide times** when planning your visit: often at low tide, the birds will be far out of sight on the mud, at high tide they may have flown off to roost. Remember it is tide times, not night or day, that govern the movements of birds in these habitats. Plan to visit on a rising (preferably) or falling tide for best views, or locate high-tide roosts by watching the flight-lines of waders heading for them — then you could get excellent views. In inland habitats like woodland, again a **knowledge of behaviour** can help. Birds tend to be active soon after dawn and before dusk, and in summer these are good times to see the singers, and most usefully, become familiar with their songs. In winter, many birds will gather just before dusk to go to roost. In contrast, the middle hours of the day can often be relatively quiet, with few birds moving, especially in a hot summer.

The **hides** which are a feature of many nature reserves often give excellent views and help you to become familiar with the birds of a particular habitat, and to gain an insight into their daily lives. It is easy to forget that a car, strategically parked, can provide similarly good views; or that our homes offer a privileged view of the birds nearby, especially if the garden has some drinking water and plenty of food both on the bird table and in the form of berried shrubs and other food plants. An amazing range of birds can visit even the average suburban garden.

Although fieldcraft is all about getting close to birds without causing disturbance, always remember to put the birds' interests first. Nesting birds not only demand special consideration, but are mostly protected by law, not just from egg collectors but from any disturbance. By all means watch and enjoy garden birds' nests or follow the progress of tit families using **nestboxes**. A bicycle mirror fixed to a stick allows you a good view of the nest and contents without leaving a tell-tale track through the surrounding vegetation. If the parent is sitting, pass quietly by and come back later. The **Birdwatchers' Code** also requires that special consideration is given to newly arrived migrants, tired after a long journey, and to all birds during severe winter weather. In both cases it is vital that they can feed uninterrupted, so remember their needs and do not be overanxious for a good view. And of course, obey the **Country Code**, leaving gates shut, keeping to footpaths, controlling dogs, causing no fires and leaving no litter. In essence, respect and protect the whole countryside as a valuable asset.

RED-THROATED DIVER *Gavia stellata*

Large (55 cm), slender-bodied diving waterbird, well streamlined for swimming. Watch for slim, pale, upturned beak. Looks hump-backed in flight, with rapid deep wingbeats. Throat often looks blackish. In winter grey, flecked white above, white below. Sexes similar.

Juvenile	As winter adult.
Range & habitat	Breeds on N European coasts and moorland lakes, winters on coastal seas, also on fresh waters.
Nest	Always close to water.
Voice	Cackling calls, breeding season only.
General	Widespread in habitat, never numerous. Black-throated Diver (*G. arctica*): straighter dark beak; Great Northern Diver (*G. immer*): heavy angular head, massive beak.

GREAT CRESTED GREBE *Podiceps cristatus*

Medium (45 cm), slim, slender-necked diving waterbird. Chestnut and black ruff and crest reduced to black crown in winter. Hump-backed in flight, showing white wing patches. In winter, pale grey back, with black, not yellow, dagger-like beak. Sexes similar.

Juvenile Chick grey with black stripes; later as winter adult.
Range & Widespread except in far N; breeds and winters on
habitat large fresh waters; also winters on sea.
Nest Raft of waterweed moored to reeds.
Voice Guttural croaks and honks in summer.
General Rarer Red-necked Grebe (*P. grisegena*): smaller, with rufous neck and white cheeks in summer, grey with whitish cheeks in winter.

LITTLE GREBE   *Tachybaptus ruficollis*

Smallest grebe (25 cm). A dark and dumpy diving waterbird, short-necked and tail-less in appearance. Chestnut throat often appears blackish. Watch for short dark beak, pale-tipped in summer. In winter, dull brown above, paler below. Rarely flies far except at night, escapes threats by submerging. Sexes similar.

Juvenile Chick grey with black stripes; later as winter adult.

Range & habitat Widespread except far N; breeds and winters on fresh well-vegetated waters; some winter on sheltered coastal seas.

Nest Raft of waterweed, moored to reeds.

Voice Far-carrying whinnying, usually when breeding.

General Commonest and most widespread grebe.

FULMAR   *Fulmarus glacialis*

Medium seabird (45 cm), superficially gull-like, but actually a petrel. Watch for dumpy but well-streamlined body, dark eyes, and stubby yellow beak with tubular nostrils. Distinctive flight on short, straight all-pale wings, often held slightly downcurved. Glides often, with only occasional wingbeats except near cliffs. Sexes similar.

Juvenile As adult.
Range & habitat Breeds colonially on N and W coasts, usually on cliffs; winters in coastal and oceanic seas.
Nest Single large egg laid on bare ground.
Voice Cackles and croons on breeding ledges.
General Widespread, locally common; a successful bird, spreads and colonizes new areas, even on buildings.

GANNET *Sula bassana*

Huge (90 cm) unmistakable seabird. Watch for white, cigar-shaped body and long straight, slender, black-tipped wings. In summer, yellow head of adult inconspicuous. Plunges spectacularly for fish. Sexes similar.

Juvenile	Grey-brown, flecked white becoming whiter, reaches adult plumage after three years.
Range & habitat	Breeds colonially on cliffs on N and W coasts, dispersing to winter at sea.
Nest	Mound of seaweed on bare rocky ledge.
Voice	Harsh honks and grating calls at colony.
General	Widespread, but breeding colonies few though sometimes enormous.

CORMORANT   *Phalacrocorax carbo*

Huge (90 cm), dark, broad-winged seabird. Watch for thick-necked, heavy-beaked appearance; whitish face of breeding adult. Swims well, diving frequently, emerging to dry wings in heraldic stance. Flies straight, often in groups in V formation. Sexes similar.

Juvenile	Dark brown above with paler underside.
Range & habitat	Breeds colonially on most rocky coasts, occasionally in trees beside large fresh waters. Winters on coastal seas and larger inland waters.
Nest	Untidy mound of seaweed and flotsam on rocks.
Voice	Deep grunts at colony.
General	Widespread in most coastal waters, including shallow muddy bays and estuaries avoided by Shags.

SHAG   *Phalacrocorax aristotelis*

Large (75 cm), dark, slim-bodied seabird often with greenish sheen. Watch for slender neck and comparatively slim but hooked beak. Has tufted crest in spring. Lacks white patches of Cormorant (p.22), but has yellow gape. Swims well, diving frequently. Sexes similar.

Juvenile	Dark brown above, unlike Cormorant only slightly paler on underparts.
Range & habitat	Breeds colonially on rocky coasts. Winters on coastal seas, rarely on inland fresh waters.
Nest	Bulky and untidy mound of seaweed, often under rocky overhang.
Voice	Harsh grunts at colony.
General	Widespread, but usually less numerous than Cormorant, favouring deeper and clearer sea.

BITTERN   *Botaurus stellaris*

Large (75 cm), extremely well-camouflaged, brown heron. Finely streaked and mottled plumage strikingly beautiful at close range. Watch for short, dagger-shaped beak and hunched posture. Despite its size, slips imperceptibly and silently between reed stems: if disturbed, freezes in upright posture. Sexes similar.

Juvenile	As adult, but duller.
Range & habitat	Year-round resident much of central Europe, summer visitor further N. Favours large freshwater reedbeds.
Nest	Reed platform among the reeds.
Voice	Distinctive 'foghorn' booming in breeding season.
General	Inconspicuous, more often heard than seen. Declining in numbers in N and W of range.

NIGHT HERON *Nycticorax nycticorax*

Large (60 cm), dumpy heron. Watch for fine white crest, yellowish legs and distinctive two-tone dark greenish-grey and pale suede-grey back and wings. Flight silent, like a gigantic moth. Feeds at the waters' edge. Sexes similar.

Juvenile White below, heavily streaked with brown; brownish above with distinctive large white teardrop spots.

Range & habitat Summer visitor, breeding colonially in S European freshwater marshlands.

Nest Bulky, in bushes overhanging water, often with other herons.

Voice Usually silent; some harsh shrieks at colony.

General Large eyes for crepuscular life: roosts in trees during the day, flies at dusk to wetland feeding areas. Quite common in breeding areas, scarce vagrant elsewhere.

LITTLE EGRET *Egretta garzetta*

Large (55 cm), slim, all-white heron. Watch for black dagger-like beak, black legs with yellow feet distinctive in flight. Breeding adult has fine filamentous summer plumes on throat and back. Sexes similar.

Juvenile	Duller white, lacking plumes.
Range & habitat	Summer visitor, breeding colonially in S European wetlands, sometimes resident year-round.
Nest	Bulky, in trees overhanging water.
Voice	Honks and shrieks in breeding season.
General	Locally quite common. Rare Great White Egret (*E. alba*): larger, with heavy yellow beak. Scarce Cattle Egret (*Bubulcus ibis*): dumpy, with yellow beak and legs. Squacco Heron (*Ardeola ralloides*): brown-streaked crown and buff back contrasting with white wings. All largely restricted to S Europe.

GREY HERON *Ardea cinerea*

Huge (90 cm), long-legged, long-necked heron. Broad,
heavily fingered wings and ponderous flight, legs
outstretched but neck folded back between shoulders.
Paces slowly through shallow water, stabbing fish and other
prey. Yellow dagger-like beak may be orange in summer,
when plumes on neck and back conspicuous. Sexes similar.

Juvenile As adult, but drabber, no crest or plumes.
Range & Year-round resident or migrant over much of Europe,
habitat summer visitor to N and E. Favours lakes or
marshland; in winter also coasts and garden ponds.
Nest Bulky, in trees or reedbeds.
Voice Amazing cacophony of honks and shrieks at nest,
elsewhere typically *frank* if disturbed.
General Widespread throughout Europe.

PURPLE HERON *Ardea purpurea*

Huge (80 cm), slim, dark heron, long-legged, long-necked and broad winged. Slender sinuous chestnut and black neck, and chestnut and grey back plumes in summer. Yellowish dagger-like beak seems disproportionately large. Looks dark in flight. Secretive. Sexes similar.

Juvenile	Upperparts rich brown, paler below, lacking distinctive black streaking and plumes of adult.
Range & habitat	Summer visitor, mainly to S European freshwater marshlands; breeds colonially in reedbeds.
Nest	Broad reed platform in reedbed.
Voice	Rarely heard harsh *ark*.
General	Locally quite common in the S, favouring extensive reedbeds. Occasional birds venture N, some breeding in the Low Countries.

WHITE STORK *Ciconia ciconia*

Huge (100 cm) and superficially heron-like with long neck
and legs and powerful dagger-like beak, but storks fly neck
outstretched on broad, heavily fingered wings. Black and
dirty-white plumage: breeding adult has shaggy throat
feathers in summer. Sexes similar.

Juvenile As drab adult, brown beak and legs.
Range & habitat Summer visitor to SW and central/NE Europe, feeds
fields, marshland, nests in trees or buildings.
Nest Conspicuously bulky.
Voice Rarely vocal: grunts and hisses at nest.
General Beak clattering displays between pairs at nest more
than compensate for lack of true vocalization.
Migrates in flocks over long-established routes.
Regular in breeding areas, scarce elsewhere.

SPOONBILL *Platalea leucorodia*

Huge (80 cm), long-legged, long-necked waterbird with distinctive beak and feeding technique as it sifts through mud and shallows in search of molluscs. All-white plumage, legs and beak black. Usually flies in groups, necks outstretched, in V-formation. Sexes similar.

Juvenile As drab adult, but with black wingtips conspicuous in flight.

Range & habitat Summer visitor to widely separated major wetlands in SW, north-central, and SE Europe. Feeds in fresh, brackish or saline waters.

Nest Breeds colonially, usually on reed platforms in extensive reedbeds.

Voice Rarely vocal: grunts at nest.

General Regular at breeding sites; vagrant elsewhere.

GREATER FLAMINGO *Phoenicopterus ruber*

Huge (125 cm), unmistakable waterbird, with very long pink legs and long neck, held outstretched in flight when rich pink wings show to best effect. Usually in flocks, flies in loose V-formation. Distinctive banana-shaped beak is held upside down under water, filtering out food.

Juvenile	Greyer, pink after a year or two.
Range &	Year-round resident or short-haul migrant to breeding
habitat	areas in S Spain and France. Favours extensive, usually shallow, saline or brackish lagoons with mudflats.
Nest	Like miniature volcano, built of mud.
Voice	Goose-like honks and cackles.
General	Locally common near breeding sites, vagrant elsewhere. Other flamingo species regularly escape from waterfowl collections, and may turn up anywhere.

MUTE SWAN *Cygnus olor*

Huge (150 cm) and familiar. Watch for S-curved neck and orange-red beak with black knob more prominent in male. Arches wings like sails in defence of territory or young. In flight, broad all-white wings produce distinctive creaking sound. Long pattering take-off run. Sexes broadly similar.

Juvenile As adult, but grey-buff.

Range & Widespread across N and W Europe, summer visitor
habitat in N, year-round resident elsewhere. Favours fresh waters of most types, including urban areas. Occasional only on sheltered seas.

Nest Bulky mound of reeds etc beside water.

Voice Often silent, hisses, grunts in breeding territory.

General Widespread, only locally numerous. Numbers currently recovering after decline due to lead poisoning.

Whooper Swan *Cygnus cygnus*

Huge (150 cm) all-white swan. Watch for long, straight neck and wedge-shaped head profile. Beak characteristically black and yellow. Wings quiet in flight, but family parties are wonderfully vociferous. Sexes similar.

Juvenile	As adult, but pale grey-buff.
Range & habitat	Summer visitor breeding on Arctic tundra, migrant or winter visitor to NW Europe, primarily Britain and Ireland. Favours marshland, estuaries and larger fresh waters.
Nest	Bulky mound of vegetation near water.
Voice	Vocal; bugle-like whooping calls.
General	Scarce, but locally regular. Bewick's swan (*C. bewickii*): much smaller (120 cm), with short, straight neck and shorter black and yellow beak, musical goose-like honking calls

PINK-FOOTED GOOSE *Anser brachyrhynchus*

Large (65 cm), neatly-built grey goose. Watch for distinctive dark brown head and short neck, stubby dark beak with pink marking. Legs pink. In flight, grey back and forewings contrast with dark flight feathers. Sexes similar.

Juvenile	Similar to adult.
Range & habitat	Breeds on tundra, usually on rocky outcrops. Winters across NW Europe on fresh and salt marshland, open farmland, often roosting on large lakes.
Nest	Down-lined cup on ground.
Voice	Vocal; distinctive *wink-wink-wink*.
General	Locally numerous. Scarcer Bean Goose (*A. fabalis*): similar, but larger (75 cm), longer necked, with large, dark, wedge-shaped beak with yellow markings, legs orange.

WHITE-FRONTED GOOSE *Anser albifrons*

Large (70 cm), grey goose. Watch for adult's white forehead and blackish barring on breast. Beak pink (Russian race) or orange-yellow (Greenland race). In flight shows uniformly grey-brown wings with darker flight feathers. Sexes similar.

Juvenile	Lacks white face and black barring.
Range & habitat	Breeds on high Arctic tundra, winters on NW and extreme SE European coastal and sometimes inland marshes and open farmland.
Nest	Down-lined cup on ground.
Voice	Vocal; high-pitched, musical yelping.
General	Fairly widespread, usually in flocks and locally numerous. Rare Lesser White-fronted Goose (*A. erythropus*): smaller, with more white on head and yellow eye-ring.

GREYLAG GOOSE *Anser anser*

Largest (80 cm) and heaviest-built of the grey geese.
Watch for thick neck and dark brown head, pink legs and
heavy pink (eastern race) or orange (western) beak. In
flight shows pale grey forewing patches. Sexes similar.

Juvenile	As dull adult with brown beak and legs.
Range & habitat	Summer visitor, year-round resident or winter visitor in NW Europe, winter visitor in S. Breeds on moorland and tundra, winters on farmland and coastal marshes. May roost on freshwater lakes.
Nest	Bulky, down-lined cup on ground.
Voice	Vocal; cackling and gabbling calls indicate its ancestry of the farmyard goose.
General	Fairly widespread, frequently introduced by man. Locally numerous.

CANADA GOOSE *Branta canadensis*

Largest (75 cm) black goose. Watch for long black neck and head with white chin patch. In flight, uniformly scaly brown wings contrast with black and white rump and tail. Sexes similar.

Juvenile Resembles dull adult.

Range & habitat Occasional vagrants from N America winter with grey geese on marshland. Most European birds (NW and W areas) derive from stock introduced by waterfowl enthusiasts and are year-round residents on larger fresh waters and adjacent grassland.

Nest Bulky down-lined cup, usually near water.

Voice Strident *aah-honk.*

General Though restricted to a handful of NW European countries, is increasing in numbers and spreading.

BRENT GOOSE *Branta bernicla*

Large (60 cm), very dark goose. Looks short necked, with stubby beak. Adult has white collar mark. Breast grey in extreme W birds, blackish elsewhere. Watch for all-black neck and wings contrasting with white rump in flight. Sexes similar.

Juvenile As adult, white bars on back and wings.

Range & habitat Breeds on high Arctic tundra, winters on W estuaries, sheltered bays and nearby fields.

Nest Down-lined cup on ground near sea.

Voice Vocal; grumbling *rrruk*.

General Local, but often numerous winter visitor. Barnacle Goose (*B. leucopsis*): similar size, scaly grey back, white belly and white face contrast with black neck. Winter visitor, favours coastal grassland.

SHELDUCK   *Tadorna tadorna*

Large (60 cm), rather long-necked goose-like duck with unmistakable black, white and chestnut plumage. Looks pied at a distance and in flight, when chestnut areas are less conspicuous. Sexes similar, but drake has knob on red beak, duck may have white face patch in summer.

Juvenile Duckling striped black-and-white, immature greyish above, white below.

Range & habitat Summer visitor to S Scandinavia, year-round resident in W, winter visitor further S. Favours estuaries and sheltered sandy or muddy bays, occasional inland.

Nest Usually concealed in burrow, deserted building or dense vegetation; down-lined.

Voice Whistles and barking *ack-ack*.

General Widespread coastally, often numerous.

WIGEON   *Anas penelope*

Medium (45 cm), surface-feeding duck. Drake handsome, duck subdued in camouflage plumage of distinctive cinnamon browns. In flight, both sexes show green speculum; duck shows distinctive white belly, drake bold white patches on inner half of wing.

Juvenile	Resembles female, as does eclipse male.
Range &	Summer visitor to N, breeding beside tundra pools.
habitat	Winter visitor to much of central and S Europe, occurring on lakes, marshes, estuaries and coastal seas.
Nest	Well-concealed, down-lined grass cup on ground.
Voice	Drake has characteristic piercing whistle; duck a soft, low purr.
General	Widespread and often common in winter.

GADWALL   *Anas strepera*

Large (50 cm), surface-feeding duck, apparently drab
except at close range, when beautiful detail is apparent.
Drake appears overall dull grey, duck well-camouflaged in
browns. Watch for black undertail (drake) and distinctive
black and white speculum in both sexes in flight.

Juvenile   Resembles female, as does eclipse male.
Range &   Year-round resident in some central and W areas,
habitat   summer visitor to N, winter visitor to S Europe.
Breeds on marshland beside large fresh waters;
winters in similar areas and on estuaries and
sheltered coastal waters.
Nest   Well-concealed, down-lined grass cup on ground.
Voice   Rare; drake whistles softly, duck quacks.
General   Widespread, rarely numerous, but increasing.

TEAL   *Anas crecca*

Medium (35 cm), but distinctively small for a surface-feeding duck. Head pattern of drake clear only at close range. Duck finely streaked grey-brown. Both sexes have white-bordered dark black and green speculum.

Juvenile Resembles female, as does eclipse male.

Range & habitat Year-round resident over much of Europe, summer migrant in far N and winter visitor in extreme S. Breeds on marshland with pools; winters on well-vegetated fresh waters, and on estuaries and sheltered coasts.

Nest Well-concealed in waterside vegetation.

Voice Drake has distinctive bell-like call and harsh *krit*; duck a harsh *quack*.

General Widespread, often common. Fast and agile, jinking flight is useful guide.

MALLARD *Anas platyrhynchos*

Large (58 cm), familiar, surface-feeding duck, the drake brightly coloured, the duck well camouflaged in browns and fawns. In flight, both sexes show purple speculum, bordered in white, on trailing edge of inner half of wing.

Juvenile Resembles female, as does eclipse male.

Range & habitat Year-round resident over most of Europe, summer migrant in far N. Seen on all types of fresh waters anywhere; estuaries and coastal seas, especially in winter.

Nest Of grass, lined with dark down, well concealed in ground vegetation, often close to water.

Voice Drake whistles quietly; duck quacks harshly.

General Widespread and common, one of the most adaptable of all birds, associates readily with man.

PINTAIL *Anas acuta*

Medium-sized, surface-feeding duck; drake's distinctively slim, long tail takes the overall length to 70 cm. Watch for white neck mark, prominent even at a distance. Duck pale grey-brown with bold, dark brown markings. Both sexes slim and elongated in flight, with inconspicuous brown speculum on trailing edge of narrow wings.

Juvenile	Resembles female, as does eclipse male.
Range & habitat	Year-round resident in central and W Europe, summer visitor to N and winter visitor to S. Breeds beside moorland and tundra pools, winters on sheltered coastal waters, estuaries and marshes, occasionally on fresh waters.
Nest	Well-concealed, down-lined grass cup on ground.
Voice	Rare; drake whistles, duck growls.
General	Widespread, but rarely very numerous.

GARGANEY *Anas querquedula*

Medium (38 cm), surface-feeding duck, only slightly larger than Teal (p.42). Drake striking, watch for bold white eyestripe, duck camouflaged in browns, but has striped face pattern (distinguishes from Teal). In flight, both sexes show distinctive pale blue-grey forewing and white-bordered green speculum.

Juvenile	Resembles female, as does eclipse male.
Range &	Summer visitor to extensive reedy freshwater
habitat	wetlands in central and N Europe.
Nest	On ground near water, concealed in dense vegetation.
Voice	Drake has distinctive crackling rattle; duck a short quack.
General	Widespread, rarely numerous: unlike Teal, occasional on brackish water and rare on salt waters.

SHOVELER   *Anas clypeata*

Medium (50 cm), surface-feeding duck, swimming low in
the water, head tilted down because of massive spoon-
shaped beak. Green head of drake looks black at a distance.
Duck pale brown with darker speckling. In flight, watch for
rapid wingbeats and head-up, tail-down attitude in both
sexes, and pale grey forewing patches.

Juvenile	Resembles female, as does eclipse male.
Range &	Summer visitor to N and E Europe, year-round
habitat	resident in W, winter visitor to S. Breeds and
	winters on marshes with shallow muddy lakes, also
	on reservoirs and sheltered coasts.
Nest	Well-concealed, down-lined grass cup on ground.
Voice	Drake *tuk-tuk*; duck a quiet quack.
General	Widespread and fairly common.

RED-CRESTED POCHARD *Netta rufina*

Large (55 cm) diving duck, but dives infrequently and behaves like a surface-feeder. Drake striking, duck brown, paler on belly; watch for dark brown crown contrasting with distinctive pale grey cheeks. In flight, both sexes show bold broad white wingbar running the length of the wing.

Juvenile	Resembles female, as does eclipse male, but pale cheeks less prominent.
Range & habitat	Year-round resident and winter visitor to reed-fringed fresh or brackish wetlands in S Europe, scarce visitor or vagrant further N.
Nest	Well-concealed, down-lined grass cup on ground.
Voice	Harsh *kurr*.
General	Uncommon, sometimes plentiful in winter.

POCHARD   *Aythya ferina*

Medium (45 cm) diving duck. Watch for characteristic wedge-shaped head profile. Drake sombre but distinctive, in grey, black and chestnut; duck rufous-brown above, paler on face, throat and belly. In flight, both sexes show greyish wings with indistinct paler grey wingbars.

Juvenile Resembles female, as does eclipse male.
Range & Summer visitor to N and E Europe, resident year-
habitat round in some W areas, winter visitor further S.
Nest Well-concealed, down-lined grass cup on ground.
Voice Rarely vocal; duck uses hoarse growl in flight.
General Widespread, locally common.

TUFTED DUCK   *Aythya fuligula*

Medium (42 cm), dumpy, frequently-diving duck. Drake has pied plumage and drooping crest. Duck also compactly built, dark brown above, paler on belly, sometimes with slight crest and small white patch at base of beak. Watch for narrow white wingbar in flight.

Juvenile	Resembles female, as does eclipse male.
Range & habitat	Summer visitor to N Europe, year-round resident in W, winter visitor in S. Breeds beside reedy lakes and ponds, winters on many types of still, fresh waters.
Nest	Well-concealed, down-lined grass cup on ground.
Voice	Rarely vocal; drake uses soft whistle, duck a growl.
General	Widespread, familiar and often common.

SCAUP   *Aythya marila*

Medium (45 cm) diving duck. Watch for finely-marked grey back of drake. Duck brown above, shading to white on belly; rich brown head with large white face-patch at base of beak. Note golden eyes and grey beak in both sexes. In flight, both sexes show bold white wingbar.

Juvenile   Resembles female, as does eclipse male, lacking white face patch.

Range & habitat   Summer visitor breeding on N tundra; in winter favours NW coastal seas, occasionally on fresh waters.

Nest   Well-concealed down-lined grass cup on ground.

Voice   Rarely vocal; drake uses low whistle, duck a double quack.

General   Generally scarce, but locally common in winter.

EIDER *Somateria mollissima*

Large (60 cm), sea duck with wedge-shaped head profile.
Dives for shellfish. Drake strikingly pied in flight, with
black belly; duck well camouflaged in browns, shows white
underside to forewing. Immature drakes blotched black and
white. Flies heavily and low over the sea.

Juvenile	Resembles female; eclipse and young males gradually acquire white plumage.
Range & habitat	Breeds on N coasts, winters S to Biscay.
Nest	Grassy cup with copious downy lining, on ground.
Voice	Vocal; drake uses loud moaning crooning, duck harsh *corrr*.
General	A typical N coastal bird; fairly widespread and locally common.

LONG-TAILED DUCK *Clangula hyemalis*

Distinctive medium (50 cm) sea duck – but one third of
this is tail. Winter drake is largely white with brown
patches (note two-tone beak); summer drake largely
chocolate brown with white cheeks and flanks. Duck in
summer is brown above, white below, with white face
patches; winter duck has more white on head and neck.

Juvenile	Resembles winter female.
Range & habitat	Breeds beside lakes in tundra of far N Europe, wintering on N and W coastal seas, very occasionally on larger fresh waters inland.
Nest	Well-concealed, down-lined grass cup on ground.
Voice	Noisy; high-pitched goose-like honks.
General	Locally regular, in places fairly common.

COMMON SCOTER   *Melanitta nigra*

Medium (50 cm), heavily-built sea duck. Watch for heavy beak, slightly knobbed and black and yellow in summer drake. Unique among wildfowl in its all-black plumage. Duck dark brown with paler buff cheeks. Flies in straggling lines low over sea, showing no wing markings.

Juvenile	Resembles female, cheeks less-marked.
Range & habitat	Breeds beside lakes and rivers on moorland and tundra in N and NW Europe, winters at sea on Atlantic coasts.
Nest	Well-concealed, down-lined cup on ground.
Voice	Croons and growls on breeding grounds.
General	Regular, locally common. Scarcer Velvet Scoter (*M. fusca*): similar in most respects, but in flight both sexes show bold white patch on wing.

GOLDENEYE *Bucephala clangula*

Medium (48 cm) sea duck, groups often dive in unison. Drake has dark head, white face spot. Duck brown above, dark brown head and white belly. Watch for bulky, angular head profile in both sexes. In flight, whirring noisy wingbeats and white wing patches are conspicuous.

Juvenile	Resembles female, as does eclipse male.
Range & habitat	Summer visitor or year-round resident in N Europe, winter visitor elsewhere. Favours marshy forests for breeding; winters at sea or on larger fresh waters.
Nest	Down-lined cup in old burrow or hollow tree; uses nestboxes well above ground level.
Voice	Rarely vocal; nasal quacks or low growls.
General	Regular in both winter and summer, but never numerous.

RED-BREASTED MERGANSER *Mergus serrator*

Large (55 cm) sawbill duck with slim, cigar-shaped body, long slim beak (with serrated edges to grip fish) and untidy bristling crest. Dives frequently. Drake subtly elegant, duck has brown head. In flight, both sexes look elongated, showing white patches on inner wings.

Juvenile	Resembles dull female, as does eclipse male.
Range & habitat	Summer visitor to far N Europe, year-round resident in W. Breeds along coasts and beside fast-moving fresh waters; winters in similar areas, at sea, and on larger inland fresh waters such as reservoirs.
Nest	Down-lined in burrow or hollow.
Voice	Normally silent.
General	Fairly widespread, regular, but rarely numerous.

GOOSANDER *Mergus merganser*

Large (65 cm) sawbill duck, slim-beaked with a streamlined, cigar-shaped body. Dives frequently. Drake strikingly white at a distance, often tinged pink at close range. Both sexes have bulky but smooth crests, giving angular head profiles. Duck has silver-grey body, white on belly, and chestnut head. Both show white on inner wing in flight.

Juvenile	Resembles dull female, as does eclipse male.
Range & habitat	Summer visitor to far N Europe, wintering in NW. Breeds beside fast-moving rivers, winters on larger fresh waters inland, rarely on salt waters.
Nest	Down-lined, in burrow or hollow tree.
Voice	Normally silent.
General	Fairly widespread, regular, but rarely numerous.

HONEY BUZZARD *Pernis apivorus*

Large (52 cm), buzzard-like raptor. Plumage variable. Watch for small grey head with inconspicuous beak and, in flight, boldly barred underwing and black 'wrist' patches. Tail usually held closed, looking long and narrow with three bold bars, one at tip, two near base. Sexes similar.

Juvenile	Variable (as adult), but browner.
Range & habitat	Summer visitor to forests and woodland over much of Europe except extreme W; migrant or vagrant elsewhere.
Nest	Bulky structure of sticks high in tree.
Voice	Rapid squeaky *kee-kee* or *kee-aa*.
General	Widespread, but never numerous. Usually solitary, but occurs in groups along migration routes.

BLACK KITE *Milvus migrans*

Large (53 cm), long-winged raptor. Watch for all-dark plumage mixture of browns and upright perching stance. In flight, watch for paler undersides to long wings, with darker patch at 'wrist'. Long triangular tail is distinctive, flexed and twisted as the bird turns. Sexes similar.

Juvenile Variable; usually paler than adult.
Range & habitat Widespread summer visitor to much of Europe except far W and N, occasionally year-round resident in extreme S. May occur in any habitat.
Nest Untidy structure of twigs, high in tree.
Voice Vocal; cat-like mewing.
General Widespread, more numerous in S and SE of Europe. Agile in flight, often in groups at carrion or refuse tips.

RED KITE *Milvus milvus*

Large (62 cm), long-winged raptor with long, deeply forked, reddish tail distinctive in flight. Watch for pale head when perched. In flight, underwings show large whitish patches near tips, contrasting with black primary feathers. Often soars. Sexes similar.

Juvenile Resembles adult, but duller and browner.

Range & habitat Widespread summer visitor to central Europe, year-round resident in S regions and extreme W (Wales). Favours open woodland and farmland, often in hills.

Nest Bulky, untidy structure of twigs etc., high in a tree.

Voice Repetitive buzzard-like *tee-tee-teear*.

General Though widespread, usually solitary and rarely numerous.

EGYPTIAN VULTURE *Neophron percnopterus*

Large (62 cm), but one of the smallest vultures. Dirty black and white plumage of adult unmistakable. Watch for yellow-tinged, roughly crested head and slender beak. In flight, note narrow pointed wings and long diamond-shaped tail. Sexes similar.

Juvenile Dark brown with rounded tail, gradually becomes whiter.

Range & habitat Summer visitor to S Europe, generally over hills or mountains, also on refuse tips and carrion anywhere.

Nest Bulky; branches on rocky ledge.

Voice Normally silent.

General Though fairly widespread, rarely numerous.

MARSH HARRIER *Circus aeruginosus*

Large (53 cm), broad-winged raptor; male brown above, chestnut below, with distinctive long grey tail and grey, brown and black wing pattern in flight. Female has uniformly rich brown body and wings, with pale creamy-white crown and throat. Usually hunts low, gliding over reedbeds, wings held stiffly in a shallow V.

Juvenile	Paler brown with heavy darker streaks.
Range &	Summer visitor to central and E Europe, year-round
habitat	resident in S. Favours extensive wetlands with reedbeds.
Nest	Platform of reeds deep in reedbed.
Voice	Rarely heard *kee-yah*.
General	Broader-winged and more small-eagle-like than most harriers. Widespread, locally quite common.

HEN HARRIER   *Circus cyaneus*

Medium (48 cm), long-winged raptor. Watch for large, white rump patch on generally brown female. Male pale grey with white rump and black wing tips. Hunts low, gliding on stiff wings held in shallow V, tail long, usually held unfanned, looking narrow.

Juvenile	Browner than female, more dark streaks.
Range & habitat	Summer visitor to N and NE Europe, year-round resident or winter visitor elsewhere. Breeds in dense ground vegetation (eg heather). Favours open landscapes including moorland, young forestry plantations, marshland (especially in winter). Roosts communally in winter.
Nest	Rough grassy platform on ground.
Voice	Chattering *kee-kee-kee*, but rarely vocal.
General	Widespread, rarely numerous.

MONTAGU'S HARRIER   *Circus pygargus*

Medium (40 cm), but small and slim for a harrier. Male like Hen Harrier (p.62), but note black bar on trailing edge of wing, chestnut streaks on flanks and no white rump. Female similar to female Hen Harrier, but white rump patch smaller; has distinctive owl-like face markings. Flight more buoyant than other harriers, wings narrower and more pointed.

Juvenile   As female, but richer-brown, less boldly marked.

Range &   Summer visitor to S and central Europe; breeds in
habitat   open habitats from farmland to marshes, moors and
sand-dunes.

Nest   Grassy platform on ground.

Voice   Shrill *keck-keck-keck*.

General   Widespread, but erratic, rarely common.

GOSHAWK *Accipiter gentilis*

Large (55 cm), heavily-built, but fast-flying hawk, larger female almost buzzard-sized. Watch for prominent eyestripes meeting on nape to give capped appearance, and fluffy white undertail coverts. In flight, note long, broad rounded wings and long tail. Usually among trees, but soars in tight circles at height in spring.

Juvenile	Resembles adult, but browner and more scaly above, buff below with heavy streaking.
Range & habitat	Year-round resident over much of Europe. Favours extensive forests or woodlands.
Nest	Platform of twigs high in tree.
Voice	Chattering *kek-kek-kek* or geck.
General	Widespread, but generally scarce. Easiest seen in spring when displaying.

SPARROWHAWK *Accipiter nisus*

Medium (35 cm), fast-flying hawk. Watch for short, rounded wings, long four-barred tail and distinct eyestripes. Upright perching stance. Smaller male greyish above, barred reddish on breast, larger female barred dark brown on breast, grey-brown back.

Juvenile As female, but streaked (not barred) on breast.
Range & Year-round resident over most of Europe, summer
habitat visitor to far N. Favours farmland with trees and woodland/forest of all types.
Nest Platform of twigs, high in tree.
Voice Sharp, fast *keck-keck-keck*.
General Widespread, locally fairly common, increasing after recent pesticide-induced drastic decline.

BUZZARD *Buteo buteo*

Large (55 cm) raptor with long, broad, heavily fingered wings. Plumage very variable, usually dark brown above, paler with dark streaks below. Soars: watch for short fanned and rounded tail, black patches in paler areas of underwing at 'wrist'. Sexes similar.

Juvenile	Similar to adult.
Range & habitat	Year-round resident over much of Europe, summer visitor to far N. Favours open country including mountains and moorland, often with tracts of woodland.
Nest	Bulky twig structure in tree or occasionally on ground.
Voice	Distinctive far-carrying cat-like mewing.
General	Widespread, locally fairly common. Perches solid and upright, on posts or telegraph poles. Visits carrion.

GOLDEN EAGLE   *Aquila chrysaetos*

Huge (85 cm) raptor with big beak and long, broad, heavily fingered wings. Adult brown, golden feathers on head and neck visible at close range. Soars frequently; watch for long, broad tail, prominent head, and wings held slightly above horizontal with upcurled tips. Sexes similar.

Juvenile As adult, but with white patches in wing and black-tipped white tail.

Range & habitat Remote and extensive mountain areas, often with forest, throughout Europe, down to sea level in N.

Nest Enormous structure of branches, used year after year, in tree or on high rocky ledge.

Voice Rarely vocal; *kaah*.

General Though widespread, always scarce. Often confused with much smaller Buzzard (p.66).

OSPREY *Pandion haliaetus*

Large (58 cm) brown and white raptor. Watch for pale underparts and white head with dark eye patches. Carries wings in a distinctive open M in flight, hovers clumsily over water, then plunges spectacularly for fish prey. Sexes similar.

Juvenile As adult, but less distinctly marked.
Range & Summer visitor breeding beside N European lakes,
habitat rivers and coasts; also year-round resident or winter visitor to extreme S Europe. Migrates over almost any water.
Nest Bulky, of branches, usually in tree.
Voice Rarely vocal; whistling *tchew*.
General Widespread, but never numerous.

KESTREL   *Falco tinnunculus*

Medium (35 cm) falcon, long-winged and long-tailed, distinctively hovers before diving onto prey. Female brown with multi-barred tail; male has black-spotted chestnut back, grey head, grey tail with black terminal bar. Usually solitary.

Juvenile   As female, but duller.
Range &   Widespread and common resident year-round
habitat   except in far N, where is summer visitor. Almost any habitat.
Nest   Lays eggs on bare ledge or in hole.
Voice   Shrill *kee-kee-kee*, usually when breeding.
General   Lesser Kestrel (*F. naumanni*): gregarious, locally common summer visitor to S Europe, breeding colonially. Male has unspotted chestnut back and pale appearance; rarely hovers.

MERLIN *Falco columbarius*

Medium (30 cm) falcon, compact and low-flying, catches prey (usually birds) by surprise and speed. Watch for dark slate-grey back and tail of male, female dark brown, paler below, copiously streaked. In flight, wings heavily barred on undersides, powerful and pointed; tail long, multi-barred in female, with single terminal bar in male.

Juvenile As female, but more rufous.

Range & habitat Summer visitor to N Europe, winter visitor or year-round resident elsewhere. Breeds on moors, tundra and rough grassland, often winters on coastal marshes.

Nest Shallow depression on ground.

Voice Chattering *kee-kee-kee*.

General Widespread, but always scarce. Can occur almost anywhere on migration.

HOBBY   *Falco subbuteo*

Medium (28 cm), fast-flying falcon. Watch for distinctive flight silhouette like giant swift with long sickle-shaped wings. White collar prominent at a distance, black moustaches, heavily barred underwings and chestnut undertail only clear at close range.

Juvenile	Brown, not grey above; buff, with dark streaks below, lacking chestnut.
Range & habitat	Summer visitor to European heathland and farmland except in far N. Often hunts over water.
Nest	Usually lays in abandoned crow's nest.
Voice	Sharp *kew* and repetitive *ki-ki-ki*.
General	Widespread, locally fairly common especially in warmer S areas with plentiful large insect prey.

RAPTORS

PEREGRINE *Falco peregrinus*

Medium (45 cm), but largest European falcon. Grey above, with finely, dark-barred, white underparts; black moustache and white cheeks. In flight, watch for relatively short, broad-based pointed wings. Circles high waiting for prey to fly below, then plunges at high speed in pursuit (stoop).

Juvenile	Brown and scaly above, buff below with dark streaks not bars.
Range & habitat	Year-round resident or winter visitor over much of Europe, summer visitor to far N. Breeds on mountains, moors or coasts with cliffs; winters on moors and coastal marshes.
Nest	Eggs laid in bare scrape on cliff ledge.
Voice	Harsh *keck-keck*.
General	Widespread, never numerous, but range and numbers increasing.

HAZELHEN   *Bonasa bonasia*

Medium (35 cm) woodland game bird. Female well camouflaged in browns, watch for male's chestnut and white flecked underparts, dark-barred grey-brown back, tufted crest and small white-bordered black bib. Often perches in trees. In flight shows grey tail with black band.

Juvenile	As female, but duller.
Range &	Year-round resident in hilly (usually birch/aspen)
habitat	woodland in NE Europe.
Nest	Well-concealed grassy cup on ground.
Voice	High-pitched trilling whistle.
General	Widespread, but rarely numerous.

WILLOW GROUSE *Lagopus lagopus*

Medium (40 cm), well-camouflaged, heavily-built game bird. Summer male mottled dark chestnut, red wattles over eyes, striking white wings in flight. Female also white-winged, duller and greyer, no wattles. Both sexes are white in winter except black tail. Remains still until danger close, then whirrs off on noisy, downcurved wings.

Juvenile	Much as female.
Range & habitat	Year-round resident of moorland, tundra and birch scrub across N Europe.
Nest	Well-concealed grassy cup on ground.
Voice	Loud and distinctive *go-back-urrr*.
General	Locally common, as is British and Irish subspecies, Red Grouse: lacks white plumage year-round.

Ptarmigan *Lagopus mutus*

Medium (35 cm), high-altitude game bird. Summer adult richly mottled brown and grey above, with white belly and wings. In winter, largely white except black tail. Watch for distinctive dark mark through eye and feathered feet, well insulated from snow. Usually run from danger rather than flying. Sexes similar except male has red wattles over eyes.

Juvenile As summer adult, but duller.
Range & habitat Year-round resident of N tundra and isolated mountain areas elsewhere in Europe.
Nest Well-concealed grassy cup on ground.
Voice Croaking *arr-arr-kar-kar-kar.*
General Restricted by habitat, rarely numerous.

BLACK GROUSE *Tetrao tetrix*

Large (50 cm), bulky game bird. Male glossy black with white wingbar and white underside to lyre-shaped tail. Bright red wattles over eyes. Female mottled grey-brown, with longish slightly forked tail. Gathers at dawn and dusk on communal display grounds (leks). Flies high, fast and far when disturbed.

Juvenile As female.

Range & Year-round resident across N and NW Europe.
habitat Favours heaths, rough grass, moorland and open woodland. Only locally common.

Nest Well-concealed grass cup on ground.

Voice Cacophonic croons and bubblings at lek.

General Capercaillie (*Tetrao urogallus*): black turkey-like male (85 cm) with shaggy throat feathers and white beak. Female smaller and chestnut.

RED-LEGGED PARTRIDGE *Alectoris rufa*

Medium (35 cm), dumpy, upright game bird. Black-bordered white bib and speckled gorget; white eyestripe and striking black, white and chestnut bars on flanks. Plain rich brown back. Beak and legs deep pinkish red. Sexes similar.

Juvenile Sandy brown, lacks head and flank patterns.
Range & Year-round resident in W and SW Europe. Favours
habitat drier farmland, heath, downland and scrub.
Nest Well-concealed grassy cup on ground.
Voice Distinctive *chuck, chuck-arr.*
General Locally common, often in small flocks. Sometimes
artificially introduced. Rock Partridge (*A. graeca*) of
rocky Mediterranean hillsides is similar, as is
Chukar (*A. chukar*) of extreme SE. Both lack the
speckled gorget.

GAME BIRDS

GREY PARTRIDGE *Perdix perdix*

Medium (30 cm), dumpy, upright game bird. Finely mottled and white-streaked grey, buff and chestnut upperparts, grey breast and dark brown horseshoe mark on belly. Erratically barred chestnut flanks. Crouches, well-camouflaged, flying at last moment. Whirrs off fast and low on downcurved wings, shows chestnut sides to tail. Sexes broadly similar: female has less marked horseshoe.

Juvenile Sandy and streaked brown, lacks marks.
Range & habitat Year-round resident over much of Europe except N and SW. Favours farmland, grassland, heath and scrub.
Nest Well-concealed grassy cup on ground.
Voice Distinctive, rusty *kirrrr-ick*.
General Widespread, once fairly common, but locally declining. Often in small flocks (coveys).

QUAIL *Coturnix coturnix*

Small (18 cm), vocal, but secretive and well-camouflaged game bird, smaller than a thrush. Underparts sandy buff, upperparts mottled browns, fawns and chestnuts, white streaked. Watch for broader buff stripes on crown and small black bib of male, otherwise sexes similar. Flies only as last resort.

Juvenile As adult, but duller.
Range & Summer visitor to much of Europe except far N,
habitat sometimes year-round resident in extreme SW. Favours open farmland, grassland and heath.
Nest Well-concealed grassy cup on ground.
Voice Ventriloquial *wet-my-lips* call.
General Widespread, variable from year to year, rarely numerous.

PHEASANT *Phasianus colchicus*

Large (85 cm, but half is long tail) distinctive game bird. Male unmistakable, rich gold and chestnut, with green head and scarlet, fleshy face patch. Female smaller, well camouflaged in mottled browns and buffs, with long central tail feathers.

Juvenile	As female, but shorter-tailed.
Range & habitat	Introduced centuries ago, widespread year-round resident across much of Europe except far N. Favours farmland, heath, scrub and open woodland.
Nest	Well-concealed grassy cup on ground.
Voice	Ringing, far-carrying *kok-kok*, followed by explosive wing claps.
General	Numbers variable as stocks artificially augmented for shooting; locally common.

WATER RAIL   *Rallus aquaticus*

Medium (28 cm) skulking crake. Watch for dull grey breast, black-barred flanks, and white underside to frequently flicked tail. Beak long, downcurved, deep red with black tip. Long legs and spidery toes pinkish. Slips silently through reeds. Flies weakly and low, legs trailing. Sexes similar.

Juvenile Darker and duller, more speckled and barred than adult.
Range & habitat Widespread across much of Europe year-round, summer visitor in N. Favours densely vegetated wetlands, swamps and reedbeds.
Nest Well-concealed cup on ground, deep in cover.
Voice Often noisy; pig-like grunts and squeals.
General Difficult to see; commoner than it seems.

81

MOORHEN *Gallinula chloropus*

Medium (33 cm) familiar crake. Watch for dull-black plumage with white flank streak and white underside to frequently flicked tail; short yellow beak and red fleshy forehead shield. Legs greenish with distinctive red `garter', toes spidery. Sexes similar.

Juvenile	Nestling has black fluffy down; immature brown above, fawn below, lacks frontal shield.
Range & habitat	Year-round resident over most of Europe, summer visitor to N and NE. Favours fresh waters from smallest pond to largest lake.
Nest	Bulky mound of waterweed, often in or over water.
Voice	Varied ringing calls, including *whittuck*.
General	Widespread, often common.

COOT *Fulica atra*

Medium (38 cm), familiar, dumpy all-black rail. Watch for grey-green legs with lobed toes, white beak and frontal shield. Aggressive, often fluffs out feathers and fights. Flies low, legs trailing, showing white trailing edge to wing. Dives frequently. Sexes similar.

Juvenile	Downy young fluffy and black; immature dark grey above, whitish throat and belly, lacks frontal shield.
Range & habitat	Year-round resident over much of Europe, summer visitor to N and NE. Favours larger fresh waters, occasionally on sheltered estuaries.
Nest	Conspicuous mound of waterweed, usually in or over water.
Voice	Metallic and strident *kook* or *kowk*.
General	Widespread, conspicuous and generally common.

CRANE *Grus grus*

Huge (110 cm), stork-like, long-legged, long-necked marsh bird. Watch for black and white neck markings, inconspicuous red crown, and bulky, bushy plumes over tail. Flies neck and legs extended, usually in V-formation, often calling. Sexes similar.

Juvenile Grey brown, paler on underside, lacking head markings and plumes.

Range & habitat Summer visitor breeding on far N marshes and tundra; migrates via established staging posts on farmland or marshland.

Nest Huge reed platform rising above swamp.

Voice Fabulous wild trumpeting in flight, whooping calls on breeding grounds.

General Generally scarce, flocks on migration.

OYSTERCATCHER *Haematopus ostralegus*

Medium (43 cm), but among the larger, more robust waders. Watch for strikingly pied plumage, stout, straight orange beak and thick, fleshy pink legs. In winter, has inconspicuous white collar. In flight shows bold white wingbars and black and white rump and tail pattern. Sexes similar.

Juvenile Dull, sooty version of adult.
Range & habitat Year-round resident, usually coastal, but also on damp meadows in W Europe; summer visitor breeding on N coasts and marshes; winter visitor to S shores.
Nest Shallow scrape lined with pebbles, seaweed or grass.
Voice Strident pipings and *kleep* calls.
General Comparatively widespread, often common; usually in flocks, sometimes large.

85

BLACK-WINGED STILT   *Himantopus himantopus*

Medium (38 cm) wader, unmistakable if full length of pink legs can be seen. Watch for jet black back and wings contrasting with white body and needle-slim, straight black beak. In winter has smoky crown and nape. Flies with long legs trailing distinctively. Sexes similar.

Juvenile Duller and browner than adult, with long brownish legs.

Range & habitat Summer visitor (occasionally year-round resident) in extreme S Europe; vagrant elsewhere. Breeds by saltpans, brackish lagoons and freshwater marsh pools.

Nest Shallow scrape on ground, lined with pebbles, shells or fragments of vegetation.

Voice Vocal; strident yelping *kyip*.

General Locally fairly common, often in flocks.

AVOCET *Recurvirostra avosetta*

Medium (43 cm), unmistakable wader. Watch for boldly patterned pied plumage and unique long, finely-pointed, upturned black beak. Legs long, blue grey. Feeds by sweeping beak from side to side through shallow water. Sexes similar.

Juvenile Greyer version of adult.

Range &
habitat Summer visitor to a few N coastal marshes, winter visitor to others and to sheltered estuaries, year-round resident on S marshes, saltpans and lagoons.

Nest Shallow scrape on ground, lined with fragments of shell or nearby vegetation.

Voice Vocal; distinctive *kloo-oot* and *kloo-eet*.

General Locally common, generally increasing. Breeds colonially, often feeds in flocks in winter.

LITTLE RINGED PLOVER *Charadrius dubius*

Small (15 cm), fast-moving plover. Short black beak and complex head pattern, with white stripe between crown and black face and forehead bar; yellowish legs and yellow eye-ring. In flight shows slim black collar, white nape, white sides to tail and lack of wingbar. Sexes similar.

Juvenile Scaly brown above, with greyish collar, pale yellow eye-ring.

Range & habitat Summer visitor to most of Europe. Favours sandy coasts, lagoons and saltpans, and inland sandpits, quarries and other excavations.

Nest Shallow scrape on ground, lined with fragments of local material. Very well concealed.

Voice Quiet, piping *tee-you*; trills near nest.

General Widespread, locally fairly common in S, scarce elsewhere.

RINGED PLOVER   *Charadrius hiaticula*

Small (20 cm), fast-moving plover. Watch for stubby black-tipped orange-yellow beak, black and white forehead, broad, black collar band, and orange legs. In flight shows broadly white-bordered tail and striking white wingbars. Sexes similar.

Juvenile	Sandier and scaly above, lacks black markings, has brown collar.
Range & habitat	Summer visitor to N coasts, year-round resident on W coasts; winter visitor to S shores. Favours sandy coasts and saltpans, occasionally inland excavations.
Nest	Shallow scrape lined with fragments of local material, on ground and well camouflaged.
Voice	Melodious *too-lee*; trilling song near nest.
General	Widespread and fairly common.

KENTISH PLOVER *Charadrius alexandrinus*

Small (15 cm), lightweight, fast-moving plover. Watch for short, slim black beak, slender black legs, black and white forehead, pale chestnut crown. Black marks on shoulders. Female and winter birds paler, lack chestnut cap. In flight shows white sides to tail and white wingbar.

Juvenile	Scaly, sandy back; inconspicuous head and collar markings.
Range & habitat	Year-round resident or winter visitor to Mediterranean coasts, summer visitor to W European coasts. Favours saltpans, muddy lagoons and sandy beaches.
Nest	Shallow scrape lined with shell fragments.
Voice	Melodious *choo-wit*, soft *wit-wit-wit*.
General	Locally common in S, scarcer on W coast, vagrant elsewhere.

GOLDEN PLOVER   *Pluvialis apricaria*

Medium (28 cm), but largish among plovers. In summer, watch for striking black-speckled gold back and white-bordered black belly. In winter, dull brown-speckled golden buff upperparts, buff breast and white belly. Flight swift, showing indistinct wingbar. Sexes similar.

Juvenile	As winter adult, but drabber.
Range & habitat	Summer visitor breeding on N moorland and tundra, winters on W wet grassland, farmland and marshes.
Nest	Well-concealed grass-lined scrape on ground.
Voice	Sad but melodious *tloo-eee*.
General	Widespread, but not numerous as a breeding bird, regular and locally fairly common in winter, often in large flocks.

GREY PLOVER *Pluvialis squatarola*

Medium (28 cm), bulky plover. In summer, black-speckled silver back and white-bordered striking black belly. In winter, dull blackish-speckled grey back and white underparts. In flight watch for black 'armpits', white wingbar, white rump and dark-barred tail. Sexes similar.

Juvenile As winter adult, but drabber.

Range & habitat Scarce summer visitor breeding in extreme N; more numerous on migration or as winter visitor to estuaries and sheltered sandy or muddy coasts along Atlantic and Mediterranean seaboards.

Nest Shallow scrape on tundra.

Voice Plaintive *tee-loo-eee*.

General Widespread, but rarely numerous, often solitary.

LAPWING   *Vanellus vanellus*

Medium (30 cm), distinctive plover, predominantly black and white, at close range black areas shot with iridescent purple and green. Watch for conspicuous long slender black crest, chestnut undertail, floppy flight on markedly rounded black and white wings. Sexes broadly similar.

Juvenile Drabber, scaly-backed with short crest.
Range & habitat Summer visitor to N and E Europe, year-round resident, migrant or winter visitor elsewhere. Breeds on fields, moorland and marshes; winters on similar areas, also estuaries and arable farmland.
Nest Grass-lined scrape on ground.
Voice Very distinctive *pee-wit*.
General Widespread, often common, often in substantial flocks.

KNOT *Calidris canutus*

Small–medium (25 cm) wader. Summer adult chestnut with mottled gold and brown back. In winter, lacks distinction: dull grey, with medium beak, medium legs and indistinct wingbar. Watch for bulky build and whitish eyestripe. Sexes similar.

Juvenile	As winter adult, but browner on back.
Range & habitat	Breeds on Arctic tundra. Brief spring migration up European coasts, but most in autumn or winter. Favours estuaries and sheltered sandy or muddy bays.
Nest	Well-concealed grass-lined scrape on ground.
Voice	Occasional but distinctive grunt.
General	Regularly in enormous flocks. Packs close together on ground and in flight, wheeling and turning as one.

SANDERLING *Calidris alba*

Small (20 cm), fast-running wader. Summer adult rich rufous cinnamon. In winter, distinctively pale: watch for short dark beak, black smudge through eye. In flight shows bold white wingbar. Chases waves in and out on the sand.

Juvenile	As winter adult, but with brown mottled back.
Range & habitat	Breeds on Arctic tundra. Brief spring migration on W coasts, but most in autumn or winter on sandy beaches and bays.
Nest	Well-concealed grassy cup on ground.
Voice	Repeated short sharp *quick*.
General	Widespread and regular, locally fairly common though rarely in large flocks.

LITTLE STINT *Calidris minuta*

Tiny (13 cm) wader. Short fine beak, black legs and grey outer tail feathers in flight. In summer, rich mottled brown above, with double V marking on back. In winter, pale dull grey, with traces of the V. Sexes similar.

Juvenile Much as summer adult.

Range & Migrant or summer visitor breeding on far N tundra.
habitat Some overwinter in W and S. Favours saline lagoons and creeks, freshwater pools and swamps.

Nest Well-concealed grass-lined cup on ground.

Voice Terse *chiff*.

General Widespread, but rarely numerous. Similar-sized but drabber Temminck's Stint (*C. temminckii*) scarcer, yellow legs, white outer tail feathers and rattling *tirrrr* call.

CURLEW SANDPIPER *Calidris ferruginea*

Small (20 cm) wader with distinctive downcurved beak. Summer adult mottled brown above, rich chestnut below. Winter birds pale grey above, white below. Watch for eyestripe and, in flight, square white rump contrasting with black tail. Sexes similar.

Juvenile As winter adult, slightly buffer, with scaly pattern on back.

Range & habitat Summer visitor breeding on Arctic tundra. Regular spring and autumn migrant and occasional overwintering visitor to W and S coasts. Favours sheltered bays, estuaries, lagoons and freshwater marshes.

Nest Well-concealed grassy cup on ground.

Voice Distinctive trilling *chirrup*.

General Regular, but yearly numbers vary greatly.

PURPLE SANDPIPER *Calidris maritima*

Small (21 cm), squat wader. In summer, mottled chestnut above, pale with dark markings below. In winter, dull, purplish, leaden-grey above, paler and grey-spotted below. Short yellow legs, black-tipped yellow beak, and white edges to black rump and tail in flight. Sexes similar.

Juvenile As winter adult, but with some darker mottling on back.

Range & habitat Breeds on Arctic tundra, winters (immature birds may be present all year) on rocky W and NW coasts.

Nest Well-concealed grassy cup on ground.

Voice Normally silent, occasional *wit-wit*.

General Scampers among breaking waves on seaweed-clad rocky shores. Inconspicuous but approachable. Regular and locally fairly common.

DUNLIN *Calidris alpina*

Small (18 cm) wader with long downcurved beak. Summer adult speckled bronze and chestnut above, white below with distinctive black belly patch. In winter, nondescript grey above, white below. In flight, watch for white wingbar and white-edged black rump and tail. Sexes similar.

Juvenile As winter adult, but generally buffer, with brown mottling on back.

Range & habitat Summer visitor or year-round resident breeding on N tundra, moorland and coastal marshes. Winter visitor or migrant to lagoons, estuaries and sheltered bays along entire European coast, inland on marshes.

Nest Well-concealed grassy cup on ground.

Voice Purring trill in flight; nasal *shreeep* call.

General Common, often numerous, often in flocks.

RUFF *Philomachus pugnax*

Medium (30 cm), long-legged wader. Larger summer male has large bright ruff of feathers. Female and winter male duller and scaly. In flight, watch for white oval patches on each side of rump and tail; long, usually orange, legs extend beyond tail. Beak orange and black in male, blackish in female.

Juvenile	Buff head and neck, scaly brown back, white belly.
Range &	Summer visitor to N Europe, breeding on tundra and
habitat	marshland; year-round resident or winter visitor in S. Favours coastal lagoons or inland marshes.
Nest	Well-concealed deep cup in grass.
Voice	Usually silent, sometimes *chuk-uk*.
General	Widespread, but scattered, rarely numerous.

COMMON SNIPE *Gallinago gallinago*

Medium (28 cm), squat, well-camouflaged wader with long beak. Longitudinal buff stripes on crown and back. Legs green, relatively short. Zig-zag flight. Sexes similar.

Juvenile   As adult, but duller.
Range &   Summer visitor to N Europe, year-round resident in
habitat   central and W areas, winter visitor further S. Favours
saline lagoons, swamps, reedbeds and wet grassland.
Nest   Well-concealed deep cup in grass.
Voice   Repeated *tick-er* in breeding season, harsh *scarp*
when flushed. Tail feathers produce vibrant
'drumming' noise in diving display flight.
General   Widespread, locally fairly common. Smaller, scarcer,
shorter-beaked Jack Snipe (*Lymnocryptes minimus*):
difficult to flush, silent, flies low and straight for short
distance, showing no white on tail.

WOODCOCK *Scolopax rusticola*

Medium (35 cm), bulky, long-beaked wader, with mottled plumage. Pale forehead and cross-wise buff stripes on angular head. Note large eyes, rounded wings and moth-like flight showing no wing markings. Sexes similar.

Juvenile	As adult, but duller.
Range & habitat	Summer visitor to N Europe, year-round resident or winter visitor to S. Aberrant for a wader in favouring damp woodland year-round.
Nest	Scrape in leaf litter on ground.
Voice	Usually silent, but in evening calls a frog-like *orrrt-orrrt* and a sneezing high-pitched *tswick*.
General	Widespread and regular, difficult to see as relies on camouflage until danger very close.

BLACK-TAILED GODWIT *Limosa limosa*

Medium (40 cm), but large and tall for a wader. Note long, straight beak. In summer, has chestnut head and neck; in winter, dull pale grey with white belly. In flight, watch for striking black and white wingbars, white rump and black tail. Sexes similar.

Juvenile	As winter adult, but buffer, with scaly back pattern.
Range & habitat	Summer visitor or year-round resident to north-central and NW Europe, winter visitor to S coasts. Breeds on damp grassland and marshes, winters on sheltered estuaries and bays.
Nest	Well-concealed cup deep in tussock.
Voice	Noisy *wicka-wicka-wicka* when breeding.
General	Locally fairly common, may flock in winter.

Bar-tailed Godwit *Limosa lapponica*

Medium (40 cm), but large and long-legged for a wader. Note long, slightly upturned beak. In summer, bright chestnut with brown-mottled back; in winter, brown with darker streaks above, whitish below. In flight, note lack of wingbar, white rump and dark-barred white tail. Sexes similar.

Juvenile As winter adult, with chestnut mottling on back.

Range & habitat Summer visitor breeding on Arctic tundra, migrant or winter visitor to W and S European coasts. Favours estuaries and sheltered muddy or sandy bays.

Nest Well-concealed scrape on ground.

Voice Rare; harsh *kirrick* when breeding.

General Widespread and gregarious, locally common, often in large flocks.

WHIMBREL *Numenius phaeopus*

Medium (40 cm), mottled brown, long-legged, long-necked wader. Long, downcurved, black beak appreciably shorter than Curlew (p.106). Watch for broad buff stripes on brown crown. In flight, note lack of wingbar, white rump and barred tail. Sexes similar.

Juvenile Resembles adult.
Range & Summer visitor breeding on N moors, marshes and
habitat tundra, migrant (often, but not always, on coast)
elsewhere.
Nest Well-concealed grassy cup on ground.
Voice Far-carrying piping whistle, several times in rapid
succession: *pee-pee-pee-pee-pee-pee-pee*.
General Widespread, regular on migration, rarely numerous.

CURLEW *Numenius arquata*

Large (58 cm), mottled brown and buff, long-legged, long-necked wader. Extremely long, downcurved beak. In flight, note lack of wing markings, pale rump extending well up back, and narrow, dark-barred white tail. Sexes similar.

Juvenile Resembles adult.

Range & habitat Summer visitor to N and north-central Europe, year-round resident, migrant or winter visitor to W and on S coasts. Breeds on moors, wet grassland and marshes; winters on sheltered sandy or muddy coasts and estuaries.

Nest Well-concealed grassy cup on ground.

Voice *Coor-lee* at all times; bubbling song in display flight over breeding territory.

General Widespread; solitary or in flocks; locally fairly common.

SPOTTED REDSHANK *Tringa erythropus*

Medium (30 cm), long-legged, long-necked wader. In summer, unmistakable, uniformly sooty black with white spots. In winter, scaly silver-grey above, white below. In flight, watch for trailing dark red legs, lack of wingbar, white rump and barred tail. Sexes similar.

Juvenile As winter adult, but buffer on shoulders.
Range & Summer visitor breeding on Arctic tundra; migrant or
habitat winter visitor on coasts of W and S Europe. Favours tundra areas close to tree limit, winters on marshes, estuaries and sheltered coasts.
Nest Well-concealed grassy scrape on ground.
Voice Explosive *chew-it*.
General Regular, but rarely numerous. Often solitary.

REDSHANK *Tringa totanus*

Medium (28 cm), wary wader. Rich brown above, streaked blackish in summer, whitish scaly marks in winter. White below, heavily brown speckled and streaked in summer, less so in winter. Note long scarlet legs, and, in flight, broad white trailing edges to wings. Sexes similar.

Juvenile As winter adult, but buffer overall.

Range & Summer visitor to N and NE marshes. Year-round
habitat resident, migrant or winter visitor to W and S coasts. Breeds in marshes; winters on estuaries and coasts.

Nest Concealed deep cup in grass tussock.

Voice Stridently vociferous 'sentinel of the marshes', shrieking calls and melodious variants on *tu-lee-lee*.

General Widespread, locally fairly common; solitary, sometimes in small flocks.

GREENSHANK *Tringa nebularia*

Medium (30 cm), pale wader. Grey back with scaly pale markings in winter, with blackish blotches and streaks in summer. Head and neck pale in winter, dark-streaked in summer. Watch for thickish, slightly upturned beak and green legs; in flight shows conspicuous white rump and no wingbars. Sexes similar.

Juvenile	As winter adult, but buffer.
Range & habitat	Summer visitor to N tundra and moorland. Migrant or winter visitor to W and S coasts and marshes. Favours lagoons and sheltered bays and estuaries.
Nest	Well-concealed scrape on ground.
Voice	Characteristically trisyllabic *tu-tu-tu*.
General	Widespread, but rarely numerous.

GREEN SANDPIPER *Tringa ochropus*

Small (23 cm), dark wader. Dark, greenish-grey back speckled white, underparts white. Short, dark green legs. Often bobs. In flight, watch for dark underwings, lack of wingbars, bold white rump and heavily dark-barred tail. Sexes similar.

Juvenile As adult, but more heavily speckled.

Range & Summer visitor to N Europe; winter visitor or
habitat migrant to coastal and inland marshes elsewhere. Breeds in swampy forest, muddy pools and creeks.

Nest Grassy scrape on ground, occasionally in deserted nest in tree.

Voice *Tloot-weet-wit* on take-off; trilling song.

General Widespread and regular, but rarely numerous. Often solitary.

WOOD SANDPIPER *Tringa glareola*

Small (20 cm), slim-built wader. Dark grey-brown upperparts with scaly white-edged feathers. Head and neck white with darker streaks, note clear eyestripe and yellowish legs. In flight, unmarked wings with pale undersides, white rump with faintly barred tail. Sexes similar.

Juvenile As adult, but warmer colour and more mottled.

Range & habitat Summer visitor breeding on N marshes and tundra, migrant elsewhere visiting inland and coastal pools, marshes and lagoons. May overwinter in S.

Nest Shallow scrape on ground.

Voice *Chiff-if-if* on take-off; yodelling song.

General Widespread and regular, but rarely numerous. Often solitary, occasionally in small flocks.

COMMON SANDPIPER *Actitis hypoleucos*

Small (20 cm), dumpy wader, perpetually bobbing. Sandy brown upperparts flecked with white in summer. Short greenish legs. Watch for whirring flight interrupted by glides on downcurved wings, low over water. Shows white wingbar and white edges to buff rump and tail. Sexes similar.

Juvenile	As adult, but duller and chequered.
Range & habitat	Summer visitor or migrant to much of Europe, winter visitor to S, may overwinter elsewhere. Breeds beside lakes, rivers and streams; winters on fresh and salt marshes, occasionally along coasts.
Nest	Shallow scrape on ground close to water.
Voice	Trilling *twee-wee-wee* call; high-pitched song based on *tittyweety* phrases.
General	Widespread and regular; often solitary.

TURNSTONE *Arenaria interpres*

Small (23 cm), stocky wader. Harlequin plumage, mainly browns and white in winter; black, white and chestnut in summer. Short orange legs and short, dark, wide beak (used to turn over seaweed and pebbles). In flight, watch for complex black and white pattern on back, wings and tail. Sexes similar.

Juvenile Similar to winter adult.

Range &
habitat Summer visitor breeding on N rocky coasts and tundra; migrant, winter visitor (or year-round) on coasts further S. Generally maritime, favours rocky, surf-washed coasts with dense seaweed.

Nest Shallow scrape on ground.

Voice Distinctive staccato *tuk-uk-tuk*.

General Widespread, locally common; rare inland.

ARCTIC SKUA *Stercorarius parasiticus*

Medium (50 cm), gull-like seabird, slim-winged, agile in flight. Two phases: brownish-grey with darker cap or brown above with white underparts and collar. In flight, watch for long-pointed, central tail feathers, conspicuous white patches near tips of brownish wings. Sexes similar.

Juvenile	Brown, speckled and barred buff, without elongated tail feathers.
Range & habitat	Summer visitor breeding colonially on N coasts, islands and tundra; migrant elsewhere. Maritime, except nesting; favours inshore waters.
Nest	Grass cup on ground.
Voice	Harsh *kee-aar* over colonies.
General	Widespread, but numerous only near colonies. Pirates fish from other seabirds.

GREAT SKUA *Stercorarius skua*

Large (60 cm) skua, uniformly dark brown flecked and streaked white and buff. In flight, is piratical (even chases Gannets (p.21)); has striking white patches at base of primaries. Sexes similar.

Juvenile Similar to adult.

Range & habitat Summer visitor breeding colonially on N islands, moors and tundra. Migrant or occasional winter visitor elsewhere. Maritime, favours coastal seas.

Nest Bulky grass cup on ground, fiercely defended.

Voice At colony only, barking *tuk* or *uk-uk-uk,* nasal *skeer.* Locally numerous only at colonies, which are few.

General Regular but quite scarce except near breeding colonies.

BLACK-HEADED GULL *Larus ridibundus*

Medium (35 cm) gull. In summer, watch for dark chocolate hood, red beak and legs. In winter, head white with black smudge behind eye. In flight shows all-black wingtips and diagnostic white leading edge to wing. Sexes similar.

Juvenile As winter adult, but with brown W mark across wings and black tip to tail.

Range & habitat Summer visitor to N and NE, year-round resident or winter visitor elsewhere. Breeds colonially on islands, dunes, sheltered coasts and beside moorland lakes. Occurs in almost any habitat.

Nest Tall mound of grass and flotsam.

Voice Yelping *keeer* and laughing *kwaar* calls.

General Widespread, common. Scarcer Mediterranean Gull (*L. melanocephalus*): black hood and all-white wingtips, more robust.

LESSER BLACK-BACKED GULL *Larus fuscus*

Large (53 cm) gull. Watch for yellow legs and, in flight, for black and white tips to dark grey wings. Head and neck flecked with grey in winter. Sexes similar.

Juvenile Speckled dark brown above, paler below, all-dark primaries. Adult plumage after 3 years.

Range & habitat Summer visitor breeding colonially on far N cliff-tops, islands, dunes and moors. Year-round resident or migrant along W coasts, winter visitor in S. Occurs in almost any habitat.

Nest Bulky mound of grass and flotsam on ground.

Voice Powerful throaty *kay-ow* and laughing cries.

General Widespread, often common, increasingly wintering further N.

HERRING GULL *Larus argentatus*

Large (55 cm) diagnostically silver-backed gull. Watch for pink legs (but S race has yellow legs) and, in flight, for black and white tips to pale grey wings. Head and neck flecked with grey in winter. Sexes similar.

Juvenile	Speckled dark brown above, paler below, pale inner primaries in flight. Adult plumage after 3 years.
Range & habitat	Year-round resident or winter visitor almost throughout Europe. Breeds colonially on all types of coast, moorland and town buildings. Occurs in almost any habitat. Favours refuse dumps.
Nest	Bulky mound of grass and flotsam on ground.
Voice	Noisy, familar laughing *kay-ow* or *yah-yah-yah* and mewing calls.
General	Widespread, often very numerous.

GREAT BLACK-BACKED GULL *Larus marinus*

The largest European gull (68 cm). Note massive beak, jet black back and pink legs. In flight shows all-black wings with white trailing edge and white spots at tips of primaries. Sexes similar.

Juvenile	Speckled brown above, paler below. Note dark trailing edge and paler inner primaries in flight. Adult plumage after 4 years.
Range & habitat	The most maritime gull. Breeds in N and W on islands and cliffs. Year-round resident in most areas, some disperse far out to sea.
Nest	Seaweed and flotsam nest on ledge.
Voice	Gruff, powerful *kow-kow-kow*.
General	Widespread, not as numerous as other gulls. Rare Glaucous Gull (*L. hyperboreus*) adult has white wingtips, immature uniformly pale brown.

COMMON GULL *Larus canus*

Medium (40 cm), grey-backed gull with rounded head and smallish yellow beak. Watch for greenish yellow legs and, in flight, black wingtips with white spots. In winter, has heavy grey flecking on head. Sexes similar.

Juvenile Has speckled head, grey back, blackish wings and black-tipped white tail.

Range & habitat Summer visitor breeding on N coasts, hillsides and moors. Year-round resident, migrant or winter visitor in S. Primarily coastal, but often on grassland and fields on migration.

Nest Grassy cup on ground.

Voice High-pitched *key-yaa* and nasal *gah-gah-gah*.

General Widespread in many habitats, often fairly common.

LITTLE GULL *Larus minutus*

Medium (27 cm), but small and dainty for a gull. Watch for jet black cap, short dark red bill and legs. In flight shows pale grey upperside to wings, note dark grey underside and rounded white tips. In winter, loses black hood, has dark spot behind eye. Sexes similar.

Juvenile	As winter adult, with striking black M across wings.
Range & habitat	Summer visitor breeding on Baltic marshes, year-round resident, migrant, or winter visitor to W and S coasts. Most winter at sea, occurs on large inland fresh waters on migration.
Nest	Grassy mound on swampy ground.
Voice	High-pitched *kar-eee* and *kek-kek-kek*.
General	Regular, locally fairly common, increasing. Note dipping feeding flight.

KITTIWAKE *Rissa tridactyla*

Medium (40 cm), slender-winged gull. Watch for crimson-lined yellow beak, black legs. Wings long and slim, held angled in buoyant flight, grey with black tips and no white spots. Sexes similar.

Juvenile	As adult, but with black spot behind eye, black collar mark, black-tipped, slightly forked white tail and bold, black M on upper surface of wings.
Range &	A maritime gull, many disperse widely across
habitat	Atlantic in winter. Nests colonially on cliff ledges, occasionally on buildings on W and N coasts.
Nest	Guano, mud and seaweed glued to sheer cliff, often under overhang.
Voice	Noisy at colonies, diagnostic *kitti-wake*.
General	Widespread, locally numerous.

SANDWICH TERN   *Sterna sandvicensis*

Medium (40 cm), large for a tern, and heavy in flight. Watch for long yellow-tipped black beak, bristling black crest. In flight, grey wings show darker primaries; rump white, tail white and slightly forked. Forehead white in autumn. Sexes similar.

Juvenile	As autumn adult, with more white on crown and scaly blackish markings on back.
Range & habitat	Summer visitor or migrant along coasts. Breeds on isolated beaches and islands.
Nest	Simple scrape in sand.
Voice	Distinctive and loud *kay-reck* or *kirr-ick*.
General	Widespread coastally, erratic but locally common as breeding bird. Gull-billed Tern (*Gelochelidon nilotica*): similar, shorter black beak and grey rump. Often occurs inland.

COMMON TERN *Sterna hirundo*

Medium (35 cm) sea tern. Note deeply forked tail with long streamers. Watch for black cap and black-tipped red beak. Wings uniformly pale grey, primaries with blackish border. Forehead white in autumn. Sexes similar.

Juvenile As autumn adult, with brown markings across back and black forewing edge.

Range & habitat Migrant summer visitor, breeding coastally and occasionally inland over much of Europe. Nests colonially on beaches and on coastal, estuarine and freshwater islands.

Nest Scrape in grass or sand.

Voice Swift *kirri-kirri-kirri;* harsh *kee-**aarh*** with emphasis on second syllable.

General Widespread and fairly common, often numerous around colonies.

ARCTIC TERN *Sterna paradisaea*

Medium (37 cm) sea tern, shorter-legged and more grey-bellied than Common Tern (p.124). All-red beak. In flight, watch for forked tail with long streamers, and translucent primaries. Forehead white in autumn. Sexes similar.

Juvenile As autumn adult, with grey-brown markings across back and grey forewing edges contrasting with white trailing edge.

Range & Migrant along W coasts, breeding colonially on N
habitat islands. Unusual inland.

Nest Shallow scrape in sand or grass.

Voice Short sharp ***kee**-aah*.

General Widespread, locally common. Rare Roseate Tern (*S. dougallii*) very pale, with extremely long tail streamers, almost all-black beak.

LITTLE TERN *Sterna albifrons*

Small (22 cm), stubby sea tern with distinctive flicking flight. Watch for shallowly forked tail, black-tipped yellow beak, yellow legs and white forehead patch. In flight shows conspicuously black outer primaries. Sexes similar.

Juvenile	Scaly-backed version of autumn adult.
Range & habitat	Migrant along W and S coasts and lagoons, breeds in loose colonies on sandy beaches.
Nest	Shallow scrape in sand.
Voice	High-pitched *kitick,* hurried *kirri-kirri- kirrick.*
General	Widespread and regular, but nowhere numerous.

BLACK TERN *Chlidonias niger*

Small (25 cm), unmistakable when breeding, grey-winged,
sooty black-bodied marsh tern. Note white undertail
coverts. Watch for black beak and legs and shallowly
forked tail. In flight, dips to pick food off water. In autumn
and winter, white body, nape and forehead, black crown
and dark vertical half-collar marks. Sexes similar.

Juvenile	As winter adult, but scaly above.
Range & habitat	Migrant and summer visitor to S, central and E Europe, breeds colonially on freshwater swamps and marshes. Migrates along coasts and over inland waters.
Nest	Semi-floating platform of waterweed.
Voice	Rarely heard *krit* or *kreek*.
General	Reasonably widespread, regular, locally fairly common.

GUILLEMOT *Uria aalge*

Medium (40 cm) auk, upright on land, swims low in the sea, diving frequently. Watch for dagger-like beak, chocolate brown upperparts. In winter, sooty black above, white throat and face. Sexes similar.

Juvenile	Resembles winter adult.
Range &	At sea for much of year off N and W Europe; breeds
habitat	colonially on cliff ledges.
Nest	Single egg laid on bare open rock ledge.
Voice	Grumbling growls and croons on ledges, silent elsewhere.
General	Locally common along rocky breeding coasts in summer, scarce and erratic elsewhere. Black Guillemot (*Cepphus grylle*) of NW coasts and adjacent seas is all-black with striking white wing patches in summer; grey backed, white elsewhere in winter. Note vermillion legs.

RAZORBILL *Alca torda*

Medium (40 cm), squat, thick-necked auk, jet black above, white below. Dives frequently. Watch for deep flat beak with white vertical line and fine white stripe leading from beak to eye. Winter birds duller, with white face and throat. Flight whirring low over sea. Sexes similar.

Juvenile	As winter adult, greyer with slimmer beak.
Range &	Summer visitor breeding in loose colonies on W and
habitat	N cliffs, winters at sea.
Nest	Single egg laid on bare rock in cavity.
Voice	Low growls.
General	Locally common along rocky breeding coasts in summer, scarce and erratic elsewhere. Arctic-breeding Little Auk (*Plautus alle*): half the size of Razorbill, black above and on throat, white on belly, small triangular beak. Irregular in winter.

PUFFIN *Fratercula arctica*

Medium (30 cm), squat, upright and familiar auk. Watch for black back, white belly and face patch, bright orange legs and webbed feet, and colourful parrot-like beak. Winter birds duller, with grey face and smaller, dark beak. Sexes similar.

Juvenile Greyer version of winter adult with slimmer dark beak.

Range & Summer visitor breeding colonially on remote
habitat headlands and islands in W and N Europe, winters out at sea.

Nest Single egg laid down burrow.

Voice Low growls.

General Locally common, sometimes numerous, on breeding coasts in summer. Scarce and erratic elsewhere.

STOCK DOVE *Columba oenas*

Medium (33 cm), dull-grey pigeon. Watch for pinkish flush on breast and metallic green collar marks. Swift, direct flight showing triangular black-bordered grey wings and dark-tipped grey tail. Sexes similar.

Juvenile	As adult, but duller, lacking collar marks.
Range &	Year-round resident over much of Europe, summer
habitat	visitor to N and NE. Mainly on farmland and woodland, occasionally on coasts and marshes.
Nest	In hollow tree or burrow.
Voice	Booming *coo-oo* or *coo-roo-oo*.
General	Widespread, locally fairly common. Rock Dove (*C. livia*, ancestor of town and racing pigeons): similar, with double black wingbars and conspicuous white rump. On remote rocky N coasts and S mountains; scarce.

WOODPIGEON *Columba palumbus*

Medium (40 cm), cumbersome pigeon. Watch for pink breast, white collar marks and diagnostic white bar visible in closed wing, conspicuous in flight. Flight fast, but noisy and clumsy, often colliding with vegetation. Gregarious. Sexes similar.

Juvenile As adult, but lacks collar marks.
Range & Widespread year-round resident, summer visitor to
habitat N and NE Europe. Breeds in woodland and scrub, feeds in woodland, on all farmland and in urban areas.
Nest Flimsy platform of twigs in bush or tree.
Voice Monotonously repetitive *coo-coo, coo-coo*.
General Widespread, often common, often in flocks. Can damage crops.

TURTLE DOVE *Streptopelia turtur*

Medium (28 cm), slim, fast-flying pigeon. Watch for pink breast, scaly bronze back and shoulders, black and white-barred collar patches. In flight shows bronze wings with grey diagonal bars, longish black tail with narrow white borders. Sexes similar.

Juvenile Duller, browner version of adult, lacking collar marks.

Range & habitat Migrant and summer visitor, breeding over much of Europe except N. Essentially a woodland, scrub and farmland bird.

Nest Flimsy platform of twigs in bush.

Voice Far-carrying monotonous and prolonged purring.

General Widespread, locally fairly common.

COLLARED DOVE *Streptopelia decaocto*

Medium (30 cm), sandy pigeon. Pinkish head and neck with white-edged black band round nape. In flight looks long-tailed and hawk-like, shows buff and grey wings with blackish primaries. Long tail buff above, black below, showing much white on underside. Gregarious. Sexes similar.

Juvenile Dull version of adult, lacking collar mark.

Range & habitat Westward-spreading, post-1940 newcomer to Europe from Asia, colonising Ireland in 1970s. Year-round resident of Europe, except N, in farmland, parks and towns.

Nest Flimsy twig platform in bush, tree, ledge.

Voice Distinctive dry *aaah* in flight; song strident and persistent *coo-coo-coo*.

General Widespread, comparatively common.

CUCKOO *Cuculus canorus*

Medium (33 cm), slim, short-legged and long-tailed, heard more than seen. Watch for grey body, barred underparts and white-tipped black tail. Beak tiny; legs yellow. Falcon-like flight on fluttering curved wings; tail looks spoon-ended. Sexes normally similar, female rarely chestnut.

Juvenile	Mottled dark brown above, white with blackish barring below.
Range & habitat	Migrant and summer visitor to all of Europe except far N, occurs in woodland, on heaths, moors, marshes and farmland.
Nest	Parasitic, lays eggs in foster parent nests.
Voice	*Cuck-oo* and variants, throaty chuckle; female uses bubbling trill.
General	Widespread, often fairly common.

BARN OWL *Tyto alba*

Medium (35 cm), pale, upright owl. Watch for finely mottled orange-buff upperparts and heart-shaped white facial disc with large dark eyes. Legs long, knock-kneed and feathered. Underparts white in NW Europe, dark-speckled rich buff elsewhere. Long-winged in flight, legs dangling.

Juvenile Much as adult.

Range & habitat Widespread year-round resident except in N and NE Europe. Favours open woodland, farmland, heath and marshes.

Nest In hollow tree or deserted building.

Voice Usually quiet; snoring noises near nest, occasional strident shriek elsewhere.

General Widespread, nowhere numerous. Usually nocturnal, but in winter may hunt in daylight.

Scops Owl *Otus scops*

Small (20 cm), secretive owl. Finely mottled and streaked plumage in two colour phases: commonest is mixture of greys, less common is reddish brown. Watch for oblong facial disc and short, upright ear tufts. Perches upright, well concealed during daylight hours. Sexes similar.

Juvenile Much as adult.

Range & habitat Summer visitor to S Europe, year-round resident in a few areas. Favours open woodland, orchards, olive groves etc, town parks and gardens with big trees.

Nest In tree hole.

Voice Monotonous, penetrating and repetitive whistling *peeuu*.

General More often heard than seen. Widespread, but not numerous.

HAWK OWL *Surnia ulula*

Medium (38 cm), long-tailed owl, active daylight hunter. Watch for speckled back and finely barred underparts, and for rectangular white facial disc with striking black vertical margins. Hawk-like posture emphasized by long tail and short, rounded wings in flight. Sexes similar.

Juvenile	Much as adult.
Range & habitat	Year-round resident in N birch and conifer forests.
Nest	In tree hole.
Voice	Distinctive rapid series of short whistles.
General	Helpfully chooses prominent perches. Locally fairly common.

LITTLE OWL *Athene noctua*

Small (23 cm), squat, upright owl, perches prominently in daylight. Watch for rectangular facial disc with white 'spectacles', and 'fierce' white eyebrows. Sexes similar.

Juvenile As adult, but paler, heavily streaked.

Range & habitat Year-round resident over much of Europe except N and NW. Broad choice of habitats from woodland, farm and heath to suburban areas and coasts.

Nest In hollow in building, bank or tree.

Voice Penetrating yelps and *poop* whistles.

General Widespread, fairly common. Pygmy Owl (*Glaucidium passerinum*): comparatively tiny, with rounded head and pale facial disc. Hunts in daylight through N conifer forests.

TAWNY OWL *Strix aluco*

Medium (38 cm), plump and distinctively round-headed owl. Plumage finely marked grey-brown to reddish brown. Watch for circular facial disc, narrowly bordered black and buff, with two central prominent buff stripes up onto crown. Large all-dark eyes. Sexes similar.

Juvenile	Much as adult.
Range & habitat	Year-round resident over much of Europe except N and Ireland. Broad choice of habitats from woodland and farmland to urban areas with large trees.
Nest	Usually in hollow tree.
Voice	Well-known trembling *whoo-hoo-hoooo* and sharp *kew-wit*.
General	Widespread and familiar despite nocturnal habits. The most numerous owl.

LONG-EARED OWL *Asio otus*

Medium (35 cm), slim and upright owl, comparatively long-winged in flight. Plumage finely marked rich browns giving excellent camouflage. Watch for rounded head, circular facial disc with buff lateral margins and paired white central stripes. Conspicuous long ear-tufts. Eyes strikingly yellow or flame. Sexes similar.

Juvenile	As adult, but duller.
Range &	Year-round resident or migrant over much of Europe,
habitat	summer visitor in N. Favours woodlands of many types.
Nest	Often in old crow's nest or squirrel drey.
Voice	Repetitive deep *poop* calls when breeding.
General	Nocturnal, widespread, but inconspicuous, even secretive. Probably commoner than seems.

SHORT-EARED OWL *Asio flammeus*

Medium (38 cm), pale sandy-brown, daylight-hunting owl. Watch for short indistinct ear-tufts; clear roughly circular facial disc, bright yellow eyes. Distinctive bouncing flight; note pale undersides to wings and conspicuous dark patches at wrist. Sexes similar.

Juvenile Much as adult.

Range & habitat Year-round resident or migrant in central and W Europe. Summer visitor in N and winter visitor to S. Favours tundra, moor, rough grassland and marshes.

Nest Rough scrape on ground.

Voice Normally silent.

General Widespread, but erratic in distribution and numbers, sometimes locally numerous.

TENGMALM'S OWL *Aegolius funereus*

Small (25 cm), squat, large-headed owl. Brown above, boldly spotted; whitish below with brown mottling and streaking. Watch for rectangular facial disc with pale then dark borders, and for conspicuous 'raised eyebrow' appearance. Eyes yellow. Sexes similar.

Juvenile	Much as adult.
Range & habitat	Year-round resident in N and E. Favours woodland and forest, often montane and often predominantly coniferous.
Nest	Usually hollow trees or old nests.
Voice	Repetitive abrupt whistle.
General	Largely nocturnal; variable in both distribution and numbers, as in several other owls depending on availability of suitable prey.

NIGHTJAR *Caprimulgus europaeus*

Medium (28 cm), slim and exceptionally well camouflaged
finely mottled and streaked brown, buff and grey plumage.
Note short-legged horizontal stance. In silent, moth-like
flight, watch for long tail and pointed wings. Males show
white patches in wingtips and at tip of tail.

Juvenile	Much as adult female.
Range & habitat	Summer visitor or migrant to much of Europe except far N. Favours dry heaths, open (often recently cleared) woodland and scrub.
Nest	Well-concealed simple scrape on ground.
Voice	Listen for extended churring, with wing-claps in display flight. Best heard at dusk.
General	Widespread, but only locally regular, rarely numerous.

Swift *Apus apus*

Small (18 cm), highly aerial bird with familiar long, slim sickle-shaped wings. Note solid, but well-streamlined, sooty-black body, short shallowly forked tail, and large head with smoky white throat patch. Often gregarious, flying at high speed in noisy groups. Sexes similar.

Juvenile As adult, but with scaly markings.

Range & habitat Summer visitor or migrant over most of Europe except far N. Usually breeds in urban areas, feeds over any habitat, often over fresh water.

Nest Rough crudely lined scrape in roof cavity.

Voice Distinctive shrill high-pitched scream.

General Widespread, often common. Pallid Swift (*A. pallida*) of Mediterranean: similar but stockier, slower in flight, slightly paler with larger throat patch.

ALPINE SWIFT *Apus melba*

Small (20 cm), but detectably larger than Swift (p.145). Shares Swift flight silhouette and long, narrow sickle-shaped wings, but watch for sandy brown upperparts, throat and undertail contrasting with white belly. Flight more powerful and faster even than Swift. Sexes similar.

Juvenile	As adult, but duller with scaly back markings.
Range &	Summer visitor to S Europe, breeding in mountain
habitat	areas, towns and on coastal cliffs. Ranges widely when feeding.
Nest	Cavity in rocks or building; breeds colonially.
Voice	Surprisingly loud, far-carrying and distinctive musical trill.
General	Fairly widespread, locally common.

KINGFISHER *Alcedo atthis*

Small (17 cm), but unmistakable. Upperparts electric blue-green, underparts chestnut. Crown blue, cheek stripe chestnut and white. Arrow-like rapid flight, usually low over water. Tiny scarlet-orange feet and large dagger-shaped black or black and orange beak. Sexes broadly similar.

Juvenile As adult, but duller, with heavily dark-flecked crown.

Range & habitat Year-round resident over much of Europe, migrant or summer visitor in N. Favours rivers, lakes and streams; occasionally coasts in winter.

Nest Excavates burrow and nest chamber in earth bank beside water.

Voice Distinctive shrill *tseet* or *chee-tee*.

General Widespread, but nowhere numerous.

147

BEE-EATER *Merops apiaster*

Medium (28 cm), slim, swallow-like and unmistakably colourful. No other European bird shows such dazzling plumage. Watch for long-winged, swooping flight and slim, extended, central tail feathers, longish, dark, downcurved and pointed beak. Gregarious. Sexes similar.

Juvenile Muted-colour version of adult.
Range & habitat Summer visitor to S Europe, favouring open dry country. Often feeds over lakes and marshes with high insect populations.
Nest Colonial, excavates burrow in sandy soil or banks.
Voice Listen for distinctive bell-like trilling *prrewit*, often audible when birds are out of sight.
General Only locally common.

ROLLER *Coracias garrulus*

Medium (30 cm), heavy-headed, and rather bulky.
Unmistakable in flight when electric-blue wing patches are
striking, especially in rolling, tumbling display flight.
Perches conspicuously on telephone wires or twigs with a
good view. Looks dull at a distance: closer inspection
reveals beauty of blue and buff plumage. Sexes similar.

Juvenile Much greyer and drabber, but with blue wing
flashes.

Range & Summer visitor or migrant to S, much of central and
habitat E Europe. Favours open bushy or scrub country and
farmland.

Nest Usually in hollow tree.

Voice Harsh and crow-like *rack, kack, kackerr*.

General Fairly widespread, but rarely numerous.

HOOPOE *Upupa epops*

Medium (28 cm) and unmistakable. Watch for black and white striped back and wings, unusual pinkish-fawn body, long black and ginger crest (erected when excited or often on landing), long, slender, slightly downcurved beak. Distinctive floppy flight, black and white pattern prominent on rounded, fingered wings. Sexes similar.

Juvenile As adult, duller and greyer, with tiny crest.

Range & Summer visitor or migrant to much of Europe except
habitat N and NW, where occasional vagrant. Favours dry open country with trees, including orchards, cork oak and olive groves.

Nest Notoriously smelly; in tree hole.

Voice Soft, but penetrating, repeated *poo*.

General Widespread, but only locally common.

WRYNECK *Jynx torquilla*

Small (18 cm) relative of woodpeckers. Short-legged, with relatively long body. Looks drab brown at a distance, but close to note beautiful finely marked plumage. Watch for striped head and grey and buff V markings on back. Beak short and strong. Tail long, soft (not stiff as in woodpeckers), finely barred. Often feeds on ground. Sexes similar.

Juvenile	As adult, but duller.
Range & habitat	Summer visitor or migrant to most of Europe except far N and NW. Favours open land with old trees.
Nest	Excavates hole in tree.
Voice	Persistent laughing *kee-kee-kee*.
General	Widespread, but erratic and inconspicuous, never numerous.

Green Woodpecker *Picus viridis*

Medium (30 cm) woodpecker, often feeds on ground. Distinctive greenish-gold upperparts, gold rump, greenish buff below. Watch for stout dagger-like beak, red crown and black face. Male has red and black moustachial stripe, female has black stripe. Flight undulating.

Juvenile	Duller, with dense darker barring.
Range &	Year-round resident over much of Europe except
habitat	N and Ireland. Favours dry heath, grassland and open woodlands.
Nest	Makes oval-opening hole in tree.
Voice	Distinctive ringing laugh *yah-yah-yah*.
General	Widespread, locally fairly common. Grey-headed Woodpecker (*P. canus*) of E Europe: browner, grey head and small scarlet patch on crown of male only.

BLACK WOODPECKER *Dryocopus martius*

Medium (45 cm), but the largest and most striking of European woodpeckers. Plumage almost entirely glossy black, with crimson crown, more extensive in male than female. Golden eye. Watch for long-necked, long-tailed 'stretched' appearance in undulating flight.

Juvenile   Only slightly duller than adult, eye pale.

Range &   Primarily a bird of E Europe, but does occur in the
habitat   Pyrenees. Favours extensive areas of old forest of all
         types.

Nest   Excavates hole in tree.

Voice   Harsh, far-carrying *klee-oh*. Drums frequently, loud
        and slow rhythm.

General   Fairly widespread and locally not uncommon.

GREAT SPOTTED WOODPECKER *Dendrocopos major*

Small (23 cm), pied woodpecker. Watch for large white shoulder patch, multiple white wingbars, conspicuous scarlet undertail. Complex head pattern; crown black in female, with red nape patch in male. Undulating flight, perches head-up on trees.

Juvenile	Duller version of adult, note red crown.
Range &	Widespread year-round across much of Europe
habitat	except Ireland and farthest N regions.
Nest	Excavates hole in tree.
Voice	Explosive *chack*; drums frequently.
General	Widespread, often common. Middle Spotted Woodpecker (*D. medius*) of central Europe is smaller, with all-red crown and dull pink undertail, streaked buff underparts.

LESSER SPOTTED WOODPECKER *Dendrocopos minor*

Small (15 cm), sparrow-sized woodpecker. Watch for black and white 'ladder' markings on back and wings. Male has white forehead and red crown, female buffish white.

Juvenile	Much as adult, but with reddish crown.
Range & habitat	Year-round resident over much of Europe except extreme N and NW, including Ireland. Favours deciduous woodland, parks, orchards.
Nest	Excavates hole in tree.
Voice	Usefully distinctive high-pitched, repetitive *kee-kee-kee*. Extended high-pitched drumming frequent when breeding.
General	Widespread, but often inconspicuous.

CRESTED LARK *Galerida cristata*

Small (17 cm), well-camouflaged, buffish lark. Long crest almost always erect and visible. In flight, watch for sandy-brown tail with distinctive chestnut outer feathers. Spends much time on the ground, running swiftly. Sexes similar.

Juvenile	As adult, but often more rufous, with smaller crest.
Range & habitat	Year-round resident across S and central Europe, absent from N and (unexpectedly) from Britain and Ireland. Favours open land, frequently farmland and roadsides, often near habitation.
Nest	Well-concealed grassy cup on ground.
Voice	*Doo-dee-doo;* varied melodious song with mimicry, usually from ground or a post.
General	Widespread, frequently common.

WOODLARK *Lullula arborea*

Small (15 cm), stockily-built, short-tailed lark. Watch for rich brown appearance and bold whitish eyestripes, which with chestnut cheek patches give capped appearance. In flight shows black and white patch on wing shoulder and white tips to outer tail feathers. Sexes similar.

Juvenile	Much as adult.
Range & habitat	Resident or migrant in SW and S Europe, less common as summer visitor to central and W areas. Favours dry open woodland and heaths.
Nest	Well-concealed grassy cup on ground.
Voice	Listen for distinctive flight call *tee-loo-ee*; melodious song (in spiralling song flight) based on *loo-loo-yaa* phrases.
General	Widespread, locally fairly common.

SKYLARK *Alanda arvensis*

Small (18 cm), long-bodied, well-camouflaged lark. Watch for short but often visible crest. In flight shows white outer tail feathers and characteristic white trailing edges to markedly triangular wings. Sexes similar.

Juvenile	Much as adult.
Range & habitat	Year-round resident and migrant in S, central and W Europe, summer visitor in N. Frequents open landscapes of all types.
Nest	Well-concealed grassy cup on ground.
Voice	Flight call a liquid chirrup; varied musical song rich in mimicry, usually while hovering or circling high.
General	Widespread, often common. Rare Shore Lark (*Eremophila alpestris*) breeds on Arctic tundra, winters on remote coastal marshes, has yellow and black face and bib.

TREE PIPIT *Anthus trivialis*

Small (15 cm), woodland pipit. Upperparts rich yellow-buff, finely marked; underparts whitish, streaked on breast. Watch for pale pinkish legs, white outer tail feathers in flight. Sexes similar.

Juvenile	Much as adult.
Range & habitat	Summer visitor or migrant to most of Europe. Favours heaths with trees and woodland with substantial clearings.
Nest	Well-concealed grassy cup on ground.
Voice	Distinctive *teees* flight call. Descending trilling song, ending in repeated *see-ar* notes, in parachute song flight.
General	Widespread, locally fairly common.

MEADOW PIPIT *Anthus pratensis*

Small (15 cm), undistinguished, streaky pipit, largely terrestrial in behaviour. Plumage variable from yellowish, through olive to greenish-buff or brown, whitish below, copiously streaked. Watch for pale brown legs, white outer tail feathers. Sexes similar.

Juvenile Much as adult.

Range & habitat Year-round resident, winter visitor or migrant over much of Europe, summer visitor to N. Favours open landscapes: moorland, heath, grassland, farmland and marshes.

Nest Well-concealed grassy cup on ground.

Voice Flight call a thin *tisseep* or *tseep;* song an accelerating descending trill, weaker than Tree Pipit (p.159).

General Widespread, locally common.

TAWNY PIPIT *Anthus campestris*

Small (17 cm), pale pipit. Upperparts pale sandy-buff, only faintly marked, underparts whitish, flushed with pink in spring. Watch for conspicuous pale eyestripe, and pinkish legs. Relatively long-tailed, behaves almost more like a wagtail than a pipit. Sexes similar.

Juvenile	Rather darker and more heavily streaked.
Range &	Summer visitor to S and central Europe, vagrant
habitat	further N. Favours arid open areas: heaths, saltpans, dunes and marshland.
Nest	Well-concealed grassy cup on ground.
Voice	Characteristic broad tseep flight call; song repetitive, reeling *seely-seely-seely*.
General	Widespread, locally fairly common.

ROCK PIPIT *Anthus petrosus*

Small (17 cm) pipit, darker and greyer overall than Meadow Pipit (p.160), longer in the tail. Watch for longish dark legs and smoky grey outer tail feathers. Sexes similar.

Juvenile Much as adult.

Range & Year-round resident, winter visitor or migrant along
habitat much of W coast of Europe, summer visitor to Scandinavian coasts. Favours rocky coasts.

Nest Well-concealed grassy cup.

Voice Strident *zeep*; loud descending trill song in parachute display flight.

General Widespread. Scarcer Water Pipit (*A. spinoletta*): paler, with unstreaked back, unstreaked pink breast in spring (whitish, boldly streaked at other times); breeds in S and E mountainous areas, winters in S marshlands, vagrant elsewhere.

YELLOW WAGTAIL *Motacilla flava*

Small (17 cm), short-tailed wagtail. Males have yellow underparts, white-edged black tails; heads vary. Blue-headed (W, central): blue head, white eyestripe; Yellow (NW, Britain and Ireland): olive head, yellow eyestripe; Spanish (Iberia): grey head, white bib, white behind eye; Grey-headed (N): dark grey head, black cheeks, no eyestripe; Black-headed (SE): jet black head, no eyestripe. All females olive above, dull yellow below. In winter, duller and paler.

Juvenile	As winter adult, with scaly wing markings.
Range &	Widespread summer visitor and migrant. Favours
habitat	open land: farmland, marshes, grassland.
Nest	Well-concealed grassy cup on ground.
Voice	*Tseep* flight call; twittering song.
General	Locally fairly common.

GREY WAGTAIL *Motacilla cinerea*

Small (18 cm). Slimmest and longest-tailed of European wagtails. Watch for grey back and crown, white eyestripe, yellow underparts, brilliant yellow rump and undertail. Wags white-edged, blackish tail non-stop. Male is brighter yellow, has black bib in summer.

Juvenile	Paler, duller version of female.
Range &	Year-round resident over much of Europe, summer
habitat	visitor to N and NE, and to some mountain areas. Favours fast-moving fresh water, streams, rapids, weirs and sluices.
Nest	Grassy cup hidden in cavity near water.
Voice	Characteristic *chee-seek* call; trilling song resembles Blue Tit (p.217).
General	Widespread, never numerous.

White Wagtail   *Motacilla alba*

Small (18 cm), pied wagtail with silver-grey back and incessantly wagging, white-edged black tail. Grey crown, white cheeks, black bib. Female duller and less clearly marked than male. Often gregarious. Undulating flight.

Juvenile	As female, but with smoky-yellow tinge.
Range & habitat	Year-round resident or migrant over much of Europe, summer visitor in N. Favours open grassland, farmland, marshland and waterside, and urban areas.
Nest	Grassy cup concealed in cavity.
Voice	Soft disyllabic *swee-eep*; twittering song.
General	Widespread, locally common. Pied Wagtail of Britain and Ireland is dark subspecies, male with jet black crown and back. Sharp *chissick* call.

SWALLOW *Hirundo rustica*

Small (20 cm including tail streamers) and familiar. Watch for dark purplish upperparts, white underparts and chestnut face patch. Swift, swooping flight on long curved wings. Shows white in deeply forked tail in flight. Male has longer streamers, otherwise sexes similar.

Juvenile Duller, with short tail streamers.

Range & habitat Summer visitor to most of Europe. Breeds in buildings, ranges widely when feeding, often over water.

Nest Open cup of mud and grass.

Voice Extended musical twittering; sharp chirrup of alarm indicates presence of a raptor.

General Widespread. Scarcer Red-rumped Swallow (*H. daurica*), of Mediterranean: blackish cap, chestnut cheeks, nape and rump contrasting with dark back.

SAND MARTIN *Riparia riparia*

Tiny (12 cm) hirundine. Largely aerial; watch for longish curved, pointed wings. Sandy brown above, whitish below with brown collar. Gregarious. Sexes similar.

Juvenile	As adult, but sandy scaly markings on back.
Range & habitat	Summer visitor and migrant to all Europe except farthest N. Breeds colonially in sandy banks, usually feeds in flight over nearby fresh waters.
Nest	Excavates burrow in bank.
Voice	Soft rattling trill, sharp chirrup of alarm.
General	Widespread, locally numerous. Has declined dramatically in some areas recently. Similar Crag Martin (*Hirundo rupestris*): grey-brown above, grey-buff below. Heavier-built and broader-winged than Sand Martin, year-round resident in Mediterranean mountains and occasionally towns.

HOUSE MARTIN *Delichon urbica*

Tiny (12 cm) hirundine with distinctive purplish black and white plumage. In flight, watch for relatively short broad-based curved wings, white rump and short shallowly forked tail. From beneath, black cap contrasting with white undersides gives capped appearance. On ground, watch for white legs feathered to toes. Sexes similar.

Juvenile Much as adult, but duller.

Range & habitat Summer visitor or migrant over most of Europe except furthest N. Breeds on buildings, occasionally cliffs. Ranges widely when feeding, often over water.

Nest Very distinctive quarter-sphere of mud pellets, fixed under overhang. Often colonial.

Voice Harsh chirrup; unmusical twittering.

General Widespread, often fairly numerous.

WAXWING *Bombycilla garrulus*

Small (17 cm), plumply Starling-like shape and flight.
Watch for pinkish-brown plumage, black bib and face,
drooping crest. In flight shows yellow tip to blackish tail.
Red 'waxy' ends to wing feathers visible only at close range.
Sexes similar.

Juvenile As adult, but duller, lacking red feather tips.
Range & Year-round resident or winter visitor to N Europe,
habitat summer visitor to far N. Breeds in conifer woodland
or boreal scrub, winters where berries plentiful.
Nest Grassy cup in tree fork.
Voice Characteristic bell-like trill.
General Locally common in breeding areas. Erratic wanderer
elsewhere.

DIPPER *Cinclus cinclus*

Small (17 cm) and dumpy, like a gigantic aquatic Wren (p.171). Bobs, tail-cocked, on rocks before walking into fast moving water. Large white bib, belly chestnut (Britain and Ireland) or blackish (rest of Europe). Sexes similar.

Juvenile	Duller and scaly.
Range & habitat	Year-round resident in N, NW and S Europe. Favours fast-moving rivers and streams, often in hilly or mountainous country. Vagrant elsewhere.
Nest	Grassy cup, concealed in cavity or under overhang, always beside or over water.
Voice	Loud, distinctive *zit* or *zit-zit* call; both sexes produce warbling song.
General	Fairly common in appropriate habitat.

WREN *Troglodytes troglodytes*

Tiny (10 cm) but familiar despite its mouse-like, largely terrestrial habits. Watch for crouched-stance, dark-barred rich brown plumage, pale eyestripe, cocked tail and pointed, downcurved beak. Flight whirring on rounded wings, usually low and direct. Sexes similar.

Juvenile Much as adult.

Range & habitat Year-round resident over much of Europe, summer visitor in far N. Favours dense vegetation, also rocky mountains and sea cliffs.

Nest Domed grassy structure with side entrance, well-concealed in vegetation or cavity.

Voice Scolding *churr* call; amazingly loud boisterously musical song.

General Widespread, often common.

DUNNOCK *Prunella modularis*

Small (15 cm), dull bird, lead-grey on head and breast, dark brown back and wings. Beak straight and pointed, legs pinkish, strong; spends much time hopping on ground or in vegetation. Sexes similar.

Juvenile Duller and scaly.

Range & habitat Year-round resident over much of Europe, summer visitor to far N and NE, winter visitor to far S. Favours woodland and scrub of all types, farmland and urban gardens.

Nest Well-concealed grass cup in shrub.

Voice Strident piping *seek* call; brief but melodious snatches of song.

General Widespread, locally fairly common. Scarce Alpine Accentor (*P.collaris*): of high mountain areas in S Europe, broadly similar, but with speckled grey bib and chestnut breast and flanks.

NIGHTINGALE *Luscinia megarhynchos*

Small (17 cm), drab thrush. Watch for warm brown back, paler underside, relatively long rufous tail. Long, strong, pinkish- brown legs. Keeps under cover. Sexes similar.

Juvenile Paler, heavily speckled.

Range & habitat Summer visitor or migrant to S and central Europe. Prefers woodland with dense undergrowth, scrub, and swampy thickets.

Nest Well-concealed leafy cup near ground.

Voice Fluid *hoo-eet* call; song rich and varied, long and melodious; listen for opening *pee-ooo* notes.

General Widespread, locally quite common. Similar Thrush Nightingale (*L. luscinia*) in same habitats further N, greyish below, faint speckling.

BLUETHROAT *Luscinia svecica*

Small (15 cm), often secretive thrush. Male has electric blue throat with red or white central spot, much duller in autumn and winter. Female has black-fringed white throat. Watch for brown tail, darker at tip, chestnut patches on either side at base – often all that is seen as darts for cover.

Juvenile Sandy brown and speckled, with characteristic tail pattern.

Range & habitat Summer visitor to N and NE Europe, migrant or vagrant elsewhere. Prefers dense, low, swampy scrub or heathland.

Nest Well-concealed grassy cup on ground.

Voice Sharp *tack* call; extended high-pitched melodious warbling song.

General Locally fairly common.

ROBIN *Erithacus rubecula*

Tiny (13 cm), familiar, plump, long-legged thrush. Watch for rich orange-red face and breast with grey margin. Back brown, underparts whitish. Perky stance showing short brown tail, hops rapidly. Often terrestrial, flights usually short and low. Sexes similar.

Juvenile	Reddish-brown above with buff markings, whitish below heavily scaled with brown.
Range & habitat	Year-round resident, migrant or winter visitor over much of Europe, summer visitor to N and NE. Varied habitat from woodland, parks and gardens to offshore islands in winter.
Nest	Well-concealed grassy cup on or near the ground, often in cavity.
Voice	Sharp *tick* call; high-pitched warbling song.
General	Widespread, often common.

REDSTART *Phoenicurus phoenicurus*

Small (15 cm), slim, red-tailed chat. Watch for grey back, white forehead, black face and chestnut underparts of summer male, colours partly concealed by buff markings at other times. Female brown above, pale buff below, but with characteristic brown-centred chestnut-red tail. Both sexes show plain brown wings in flight.

Juvenile   Speckled, with brown-centred red tail.

Range &   Summer visitor or migrant across Europe. Favours
habitat   woodland, parks and occasionally heaths.

Nest   Well-concealed grassy cup, usually concealed in cavity.

Voice   Fluting *too-eet* call; brief, scratchy, but melodious song, ending in a rattle.

General   Widespread, locally fairly common.

BLACK REDSTART *Phoenicurus ochruros*

Small (15 cm), distinctively dark, red-tailed chat. Summer male sooty black, paler in winter. Watch for white wing patches. Female uniformly sooty buff. Both sexes have characteristic brown-centred chestnut-red tail. Often feeds on ground. Flicks and shivers tail.

Juvenile As female, but heavily speckled buff.
Range & Year-round resident, migrant or winter visitor to W,
habitat SW and S Europe, summer visitor to N and E. Varied habitat including mountain screes, town roofs and major buildings.
Nest Grassy cup, well concealed in cavity.
Voice Sharp *tack* call; brief rattling fast warbling song.
General Widespread, locally common in S.

WHINCHAT *Saxicola rubetra*

Tiny (13 cm), upright chat. Watch for bold white eyestripe separating dark crown from equally dark cheeks, white moustachial streak, and orange-flushed breast of male. Female paler and duller. Chooses prominent perches, continuously flicks wings and tail. In flight shows white patches in wings and distinctive white sides to base of tail.

Juvenile As female, but drabber, heavily speckled.
Range & Summer visitor or migrant over most of Europe.
habitat Favours open rough grassland, heath and scrub.
Nest Well-concealed grassy cup beneath bush.
Voice Harsh *teck* call; brief high-pitched warble of song, usually produced in song flight.
General Though widespread, scarce in many areas.

STONECHAT *Saxicola torquata*

Tiny (13 cm), plump, dark and upright chat. Watch for black head and striking white collar of male, dark brown head and indistinct paler collar patch in female. Chooses conspicuous perches, flicks wings and tail non-stop. In flight shows small white patch in wings and white rump.

Juvenile As female, but drabber, heavily speckled.

Range & habitat Year-round resident, migrant or winter visitor to S and W Europe, summer visitor to central and some N areas. Favours heath and scrub (often gorse).

Nest Grassy cup well-concealed on ground at base of bush.

Voice Frequent *tchack* call; brief high-pitched scratchy warble song, often in song flight.

General Widespread, sometimes locally common.

WHEATEAR *Oenanthe oenanthe*

Small (15 cm), pale, terrestrial chat. Watch for grey back, bold black eyepatch and wings of male; female browner and duller. Striking white rump and tail ending in an inverted black T mark conspicuous in flight. Fast bouncing hop across ground, flicks wings and tail frequently.

Juvenile	As female, but drabber, heavily speckled.
Range &	Summer visitor or migrant to much of Europe.
habitat	Favours open areas of heath, grass or moor, even coastal sand or shingle, rarely with tall vegetation.
Nest	Grassy cup usually concealed in hole, old burrow, or crevice in the ground.
Voice	Harsh *tack;* brief scratchy warble of song, often produced in flight.
General	Widespread, but only locally common.

BLACK-EARED WHEATEAR *Oenanthe hispanica*

Small (15 cm), terrestrial chat. Male upperparts whitish, washed cinnamon, underparts richer cinnamon, contrasting black wings. Black patch through eye, or black face and throat. Winter male much duller. Female as Wheatear (p.180), but darker head and wings. All have black T mark on white rump and tail, as Wheatear.

Juvenile Similar to Wheatear, but darker-headed.
Range & Summer visitor or migrant to S and SW Europe.
habitat Favours open arid stony heath and scrub.
Nest Grassy cup in cavity, usually on ground.
Voice *Tchack* call; brief high-pitched scratchy warbling song.
General Locally fairly common.

RING OUSEL *Turdus torquatus*

Small–medium (25 cm), but large among thrushes. Watch for dull plumage, sooty black in male, sooty brown with scaly markings in female. White crescentic throat patch clear in male, often obscure in female. In flight, look for silver-grey wings.

Juvenile	Rich brown, pale scaly markings, lacks bib.
Range & habitat	Summer visitor to N, W and central mountain areas, migrant almost anywhere. Favours upland grassland, moors, rocky mountainsides in breeding season.
Nest	Well-concealed grassy cup on ground.
Voice	*Chack* or *chack-chack* calls; song loud, simple, but melodious *chew-you, chew-you.*
General	Though widespread, never numerous.

BLACKBIRD *Turdus merula*

Small–medium (25 cm), but large among thrushes. Adult male unmistakable in glossy jet black with orange beak and eye-ring. Female rich brown, with dark-bordered whitish throat, often faintly speckled on breast. Looks long-tailed in powerful direct flight.

Juvenile	Reddish brown above, slightly paler and spotted below.
Range & habitat	Year-round resident, migrant and winter visitor over much of Europe, summer visitor to far N. Familiar in farmland, heath, woodland and urban areas.
Nest	Grassy cup in tree or bush.
Voice	Penetrating *pink* or *chink* calls; extended fluting and melodious song. Chooses prominent song-posts.
General	Widespread, frequently common.

FIELDFARE *Turdus pilaris*

Small–medium (25 cm), long-tailed thrush. Adult has grey head, chestnut-bronze back, dark-speckled ginger-buff breast. Beak yellow, tipped black. Watch for black tail and grey rump in flight. Sexes similar.

Juvenile Browner above, fawn below, heavily speckled.

Range & habitat Winter visitor or migrant to much of Europe, year-round resident in north-central areas, summer visitor to far N. Breeds in woodland, forests, gardens. Winters in woodland, often on open farmland and grass.

Nest Grassy cup in tree fork.

Voice Distinctive laughing *chack-chack-chack* calls; song a scratchy poorly-formed warble.

General Widespread, often quite common as breeding bird, migrant, and winter visitor.

SONG THRUSH *Turdus philomelos*

Small (23 cm), short-tailed, upright thrush. Familiar sandy-brown back, boldly black-speckled whitish underparts, tinged buff on breast. Medium-length and strength, pointed thrush beak. Often terrestrial, runs rather than hops. Flight direct, shows buff underwing. Sexes similar.

Juvenile	As adult, but heavily buff-speckled back.
Range & habitat	Year-round resident and migrant over central and S areas, winter visitor to SW Europe, summer visitor in N. Favours woodland, parks, gardens and other open landscapes with trees.
Nest	Distinctive mud-lined grass cup in shrub.
Voice	Thin *seep* call; song usually a series of musical notes characteristically each repeated two or three times. Perches prominently to sing.
General	Widespread, often common.

REDWING *Turdus iliacus*

Small (20 cm), dark, short-tailed thrush. Watch for buff eyestripe and moustachial streak on either side of dark cheek. Belly whitish, brown speckled, characteristic red flanks, red on underwings in flight. Sexes similar.

Juvenile	Duller than adult, heavily buff speckled on back.
Range & habitat	Summer visitor to N Europe, breeding in forests and gardens; migrant or winter visitor elsewhere. Favours woodland, open fields and grassland.
Nest	Grassy cup in tree or shrub.
Voice	Extended *see-eep* flight call, especially migration. Song, fluting notes in slow tempo.
General	Widespread, but erratic. Often locally numerous in winter.

MISTLE THRUSH *Turdus viscivorus*

Medium (27 cm), largest and palest of the European thrushes. Note pale sandy-brown upperparts and boldly brown-spotted pale buffish breast. In swooping flight, watch for whitish edges to tail. Sexes similar.

Juvenile Paler, greyer, grey scaly pattern on back.

Range & habitat Year-round resident and occasional migrant over much of Europe, summer visitor to N and NE. Favours open woodland, farmland with trees, parks and gardens. Often on open fields in winter.

Nest Bulky and untidy cup of grass and litter, usually high in a tree.

Voice Extended and angry-sounding churring rattle. Song melodious, simple and measured, often in early spring, uses prominent perches.

General Widespread, but rarely numerous.

BLUE ROCK THRUSH *Monticola solitarius*

Small (20 cm), dark thrush. Summer male unmistakable: slate-blue body, blackish wings. Winter male duller and slaty. Female duller, brown above, fawn below with darker streaks. Shy – creeps inconspicuously around rocky areas.

Juvenile	Similar to female.
Range & habitat	Year-round resident in rocky, often mountainous areas in S Europe, occasionally in towns.
Nest	Grassy cup, usually concealed in crevice.
Voice	Sharp *tchick* call; loud musical song, often from prominent rocky song-post.
General	Widespread, but rarely numerous. Rock Thrush (*M. saxatilis*): summer visitor to higher altitudes. Male blue above, orange below with white back, black wings. Female brown above, buff below.

CETTI'S WARBLER *Cettia cetti*

Small (15 cm) warbler, unstreaked reddish-brown back and pale buffish underparts. Watch for buff eyestripe and characteristically longish rounded tail, often held fanned. Secretive, heard more than seen. Sexes similar.

Juvenile	Much as adult.
Range & habitat	Unusual among warblers in being year-round resident, occurring in damp, heavily vegetated marshes, ditches and scrub in S, SW and (erratically) W Europe.
Nest	Well-concealed grass cup deep in thick low vegetation.
Voice	Very distinctive, explosive *chink*, *cher-chink* notes and *tack* calls.
General	Widespread, locally common.

GRASSHOPPER WARBLER *Locustella naevia*

Tiny (13 cm), skulking, dark grey-brown, heavily streaked warbler. Watch for dark-flecked crown and throat, unstreaked grey-buff underparts with pale whitish throat. Obscure grey-brown eyestripe. Sexes similar.

Juvenile	Much as adult.
Range & habitat	Summer visitor to much of Europe. Favours dense low shrubby vegetation.
Nest	Well-concealed grass cup.
Voice	Characteristic high-pitched extended trill, often lasting for minutes, similar to an unreeling fishing line.
General	Widespread, rarely numerous. Fan-tailed Warbler (*Cisticola juncidis*): smaller (10 cm), year-round resident of S Europe, reddish-brown, heavily streaked plumage, short cocked tail and plaintive *zee-eek* song flight.

SAVI'S WARBLER *Locustella luscinioides*

Small (15 cm), unstreaked reedbed warbler. Watch for reddish-brown upperparts and longish distinctively wedge-shaped tail. Note insectivorous beak, buff eyestripe, white underparts with buff flanks. Sexes similar.

Juvenile	Much as adult.
Range & habitat	Summer visitor and migrant to extensive reedbed areas across S and central Europe, less frequent in W.
Nest	Cup concealed deep in reedy vegetation.
Voice	Reeling *churr* similar to Grasshopper Warbler (p.190), but lower-pitched and in shorter bursts.
General	Ventriloquial, sings from reed stems. Restricted by habitat choice, but locally common in suitable areas.

SEDGE WARBLER *Acrocephalus schoenobaenus*

Tiny (13 cm), noisy, heavily streaked warbler. Watch for boldly streaked back and unstreaked chestnut rump, pale-flecked dark crown, chestnut-buff eyestripe, short wedge-shaped tail. Inquisitive. Rarely flies far in open. Sexes similar.

Juvenile	As adult.
Range & habitat	Summer visitor and migrant over much of Europe except extreme S, SW and extreme N. Favours reedbeds and shrubby swamps.
Nest	Well-concealed cup.
Voice	Vocal; rapid metallic repetitive jingling, twangy and chattering notes. *Tuck* alarm call.
General	Widespread, often common.

REED WARBLER *Acrocephalus scirpaceus*

Tiny (13 cm), slim, unstreaked brown warbler. Watch for sloping forehead, long beak, white throat and belly, buff flanks. Sexes similar.

Juvenile	Much as adult.
Range & habitat	Summer visitor to marshes and reedbeds across S, SW, central and W Europe.
Nest	Cup suspended on several reed stems.
Voice	*Churr* of alarm. Song extended, repetitive, more musical than Sedge Warbler (p.192). Similar Marsh Warbler (*A. palustris*) of central, N and NE Europe best identified by fluid musical song with much mimicry; often in bushy habitat.
General	Widespread, often locally common.

GREAT REED WARBLER *Acrocephalus*

Small (20 cm), but thrush-sized and among the larger warblers. Watch for unstreaked grey-brown upperparts, whitish underparts, bulky build and relatively large, angular head with buff eye-stripe and longish powerful beak. Long tail wedge-shaped at tip. Sexes similar.

Juvenile	Much as adult, buffer on underparts.
Range & habitat	Summer visitor or migrant to much of Europe except far W and N. Favours extensive reedbeds.
Nest	Bulky cup suspended from reeds.
Voice	Noisy; repetitive grating and metallic *gurk-gurk-gurk, karra-karra-karra* etc. Sings from reed stems.
General	Widespread, but rarely numerous; usually heard before seen.

ICTERINE WARBLER *Hippolais icterina*

Tiny (14 cm), warbler. Bright yellow breast and belly, yellow eyestripe, long beak and sloping forehead. Watch for blue legs, pale panel in closed wing, wingtips extending halfway along tail when perched. Sexes similar.

Juvenile	Much as adult.
Range & habitat	Summer visitor or migrant to central and N Europe, occasional elsewhere. Favours scrubby growth in woods, gardens, heath etc.
Nest	Neat grassy cup, well-concealed in bush.
Voice	Hard *tack* call; extended jingling song.
General	Widespread, locally common. Replaced by Melodious Warbler (*H. polyglotta*) in S Europe: brown legs, no wing panel, closed wings only reach base of tail, gradually accelerating song.

DARTFORD WARBLER *Sylvia undata*

Tiny (13 cm), very dark, very long-tailed warbler. Watch for grey back, dark red-brown breast and speckled throat. Often cocks white-edged tail. Secretive. Female slightly paler, duller and browner, pinker on breast.

Juvenile As female.
Range & Year-round resident in W, SW and S Europe.
habitat Favours dense dry heath, gorse or maquis.
Nest Well-concealed cup low in vegetation.
Voice Loud *chuck* or *churr*; brief soft scratchy warbling song.
General Locally common, but in variable numbers depending on winter weather. Subalpine Warbler (*S. cantillans*): similar summer visitor to S Europe. Red throat and breast, white moustachial streak, brown wings and tail. Brief musical warbling song flight over heath and maquis.

SARDINIAN WARBLER *Sylvia melanocephala*

Tiny (13 cm), dark-capped warbler. Male pale grey below, darker grey above, with distinctive black hood. Female similar, but browner. In both sexes watch for characteristic white throat and red eye-ring. Skulking, but active.

Juvenile As female, but duller and browner.

Range & habitat Year-round resident in maquis and similar scrub-covered areas across extreme S Europe.

Nest Neat grass cup concealed low in vegetation.

Voice Scolding chattering call; song a mixture of scratchy and melodious phrases, usually in bouncing song flight over scrub.

General Widespread, often locally common. As with other *Sylvia* warblers, inquisitive and can be drawn from cover by making soft squeaking noises.

197

ORPHEAN WARBLER *Sylvia hortensis*

Small (15 cm), but largish for a warbler. Dull grey-brown,
paler below, dark grey head, blackish cheeks and white eye.
Tail has white outer feathers. Sexes broadly similar.

Juvenile As adult, paler and scaly with duller eye.

Range & Summer visitor or migrant to S Europe. Favours
habitat open woodland, orchards, groves, parks.

Nest Well-concealed grass cup in bush.

Voice Sharp *tchack* call; song in SW race repetitive,
coarse and unmelodious, in SE race loud, fluting
and melodious.

General Widespread, locally fairly common. Barred Warbler
(*S. nisoria*) of similar habitats in north-central and E
Europe: same size, drab grey-brown, white eyes, but
dark cap. At close range, dark crescentic bars on
underparts. Melodious song.

LESSER WHITETHROAT *Sylvia curruca*

Tiny (13 cm), neat but dull warbler, whitish below with chestnut white throat, grey-brown above with white-edged tail. Watch for grey cap and blackish patches around eyes. Legs dark blue-grey. Sexes similar.

Juvenile As adult, but browner.

Range & habitat Summer visitor or migrant to central, W, N and NE Europe. Favours farmland with hedges and trees, woodland margins, scrubby hillsides.

Nest Neat grass cup concealed low in bush.

Voice Abrupt *tack* call; distinctive song: a brief warble followed by a repetitive single-note rattle similar to Yellowhammer (p.248).

General Widespread, but rarely numerous.

WHITETHROAT *Sylvia communis*

Tiny (14 cm), active warbler with distinctive song flight. Male has grey cap and cheeks, female brown. Watch for bright chestnut-brown wings and striking white throat. Tail brown, edged white. Legs pinkish brown.

Juvenile	As female, but duller.
Range & habitat	Summer visitor or migrant to much of Europe except far N. Favours heath, scrub, maquis and woodland margins or clearings.
Nest	Neat grass cup concealed in vegetation near ground.
Voice	Harsh *tzchack* call; distinctive song, produced in song flight above vegetation: a rapid but cheerfully scratchy warble.
General	Widespread, locally fairly common, reduced in W after droughts in African wintering grounds.

GARDEN WARBLER *Sylvia borin*

Small (15 cm), robust warbler, almost best identified by its
lack of distinctive features, but note voice and habitat.
Upperparts drab olive-grey, underparts pale grey-buff.
Uniformly olive-brown tail. Beak comparatively short and
thick for a warbler. Legs blue. Sexes similar.

Juvenile	Much as adult.
Range & **habitat**	Summer visitor or migrant to much of Europe, not breeding in extreme S, W and N. Favours thick scrub or dense woodland undergrowth.
Nest	Neat grass cup, concealed low in bush.
Voice	Abrupt *tack* call; distinctive song: an extended very melodious warble, sometimes considered second only to Nightingale (p.173).
General	Widespread, occasionally fairly common.

BLACKCAP *Sylvia atricapilla*

Small (15 cm), plump, distinctive warbler. Upperparts brownish-grey, browner in female; underparts whitish tinged grey in male, buff in female. Watch for jet black cap of male, brown in female. Legs bluish.

Juvenile	As female, but with ginger-brown cap.
Range & habitat	Summer visitor and migrant over much of Europe, increasingly through the winter in W and S. Favours parks, gardens and woodlands with both thick undergrowth and mature, tall trees.
Nest	Neat grass cup concealed low in bush.
Voice	Abrupt *tack* call; distinctive song: a melodious warble, briefer than Garden Warbler (p.201), usually ending with a phrase rising in pitch.
General	Widespread, locally fairly common, scarce in winter.

BONELLI'S WARBLER *Phylloscopus bonelli*

Tiny (10 cm) leaf warbler. Upperparts greenish-olive with indistinct pale eyestripe. Watch for characteristic silvery-white underparts, golden panel in wing and yellow rump conspicuous in flight. Active, usually in canopy. Legs brownish. Sexes similar.

Juvenile Much as adult.

Range & habitat Summer visitor and migrant in SW, S and south-central Europe. Favours mixed or coniferous woodland, frequently in hill country.

Nest Well-concealed grass cup, usually on or near ground.

Voice Soft plaintive *who-eet* call; song a slow, measured trill.

General Widespread, locally fairly common.

WOOD WARBLER   *Phylloscopus sibilatrix*

Tiny (13 cm), but large among leaf warblers. Watch for bright yellow-green upperparts and canary-yellow eyestripe, throat and breast, and strikingly white belly. Legs pale pinkish. Active high in canopy. Sexes similar.

Juvenile	Much as adult.
Range & habitat	Summer visitor or migrant in central, W and N Europe, and to some mountain regions further S. Favours mature deciduous woodland with scanty undergrowth.
Nest	Grassy cup, well concealed on or near ground.
Voice	Call *peeu* or *deeoo*; distinctive song: opens with a couple of *pee-oo* notes, accelerates into a cascading torrent of *sip* notes, often during song flight.
General	Though widespread, only locally numerous.

CHIFFCHAFF *Phylloscopus collybita*

Tiny (10 cm) leaf warbler. Plump, brownish-olive above, whitish-buff below, dark legs. Best distinguished from Willow Warbler (p.206) by song. Sexes similar.

Juvenile	As adult, but yellower.
Range & habitat	Summer visitor, migrant or year-round resident except in far N Europe. Favours woodland with mature trees.
Nest	Grassy dome on or near ground.
Voice	*Hoo-eet* call; song an unmistakable series of explosive *chiff* and *chaff* notes.
General	Widespread, often common.

WILLOW WARBLER *Phylloscopus trochilus*

Tiny (10 cm) leaf warbler. Yellow-olive above, yellower below, pale brown legs. Best distinguished from Chiffchaff (p.205) by song. Sexes similar.

Juvenile As adult, but yellower.

Range & habitat Summer visitor or migrant to much of Europe, breeding in far N, but not in far S. Favours woodland with dense undergrowth or scrub without trees.

Nest Grassy dome on or near ground.

Voice *Hoo-eet* call; song distinctive, a melodious, sparkling, descending, warbling trill ending in a flourish.

General Widespread, often common.

GOLDCREST *Regulus regulus*

Tiny (9 cm): joint-smallest European bird. Plump and warbler-like, active in foliage. Olive-green back, white double wingbars in blackish wings. Watch for faint black moustachial streak, black-bordered gold crown stripe, and paler patch round large dark eye. Sexes similar (displaying male shows flame bases to crown feathers).

Juvenile	As adult, but lacking crown stripe.
Range & habitat	Year-round resident, migrant or winter visitor to much of Europe, summer visitor in N. Favours all woodland, also parks, gardens and farmland.
Nest	Delicate mossy hammock high in tree.
Voice	Very high-pitched *tseee* call; song a series of high-pitched descending *see* notes ending in a flourish.
General	Widespread, often common.

FIRECREST *Regulus ignicapillus*

Tiny (9 cm): joint-smallest European bird. Plump and warbler-like, active in foliage. Yellow-green above, with golden-bronze shoulders. Watch for diagnostic head pattern of black bar through eye, bold white stripe between this and black-bordered fiery crest. Sexes similar.

Juvenile	Duller than adult, with faint white eyestripe.
Range & habitat	Year-round resident, migrant or winter visitor to S and W Europe, summer visitor to central areas. Favours all woodland, and scrub on migration.
Nest	Mossy hammock high in tree.
Voice	Very shrill, high-pitched *tzee* call; song a monotonous, accelerating series of *see* notes, lacking final flourish of Goldcrest (p.207).
General	Widespread, locally common, scarcer in W.

SPOTTED FLYCATCHER *Muscicapa striata*

Small (15 cm), drab, rather short-legged, elongated-bodied flycatcher. Dull brown upperparts, paler underparts streaked on breast. Watch for broad, but fine, black beak. Hunts by flying out on long wings to snap up insects, often returning to same perch. Flicks wings and tail incessantly. Sexes similar.

Juvenile	As adult, but speckled on back
Range & habitat	Summer visitor to most of Europe. Favours woodland clearings, farmland, parks and gardens.
Nest	Well-concealed shallow cup in vegetation.
Voice	Listen for distinctive *zzit* call; short squeaky song.
General	Widespread, but not numerous; often inconspicuous.

PIED FLYCATCHER *Ficedula hypoleuca*

Tiny (12 cm), compactly plump and distinctive flycatcher. Boldly pied summer plumage of male striking, but watch for subtler olive browns of autumn male and female. In all plumages shows broad white bar on dark wing, and white sides to base of dark tail (best seen in flight).

Juvenile	Much as female.
Range &	Summer visitor or migrant to parts of SW, W and
habitat	much of central and N Europe. Favours woodland (usually deciduous) with little undergrowth.
Nest	Usually in tree hole.
Voice	Brisk *witt* call; brief, unmelodious rattling song.
General	Widespread, locally fairly common.

LONG-TAILED TIT *Aegithalos caudatus*

Small (15 cm) with long, thin, black and white tail. Watch for fluffy appearance, black and white striped head pattern (all-white in far N birds), pink eye-ring, pinkish-buff shoulders and undertail. Flight feeble and whirring, calling constantly. Usually in groups. Sexes similar.

Juvenile Much as adult, but duller and browner.

Range & Year-round resident in woodland, scrub, heath,
habitat farmland and gardens throughout Europe.

Nest Flask-shaped domed nest of hair, feathers and moss, camouflaged with flakes of lichen.

Voice Noisy: thin *see-see-see* and low *tupp* calls between flock members. Rarely-heard jangling song.

General Widespread, often common.

BEARDED TIT *Panurus biarmicus*

Small (15 cm), tit-like, but not a true tit. Note rich chestnut-brown upperparts and long broad tail. Watch for grey head, conspicuous black 'drooping moustaches' and white throat of male. Female has brown head. Agilely clambers about reed stems. Often in groups.

Juvenile Pale, drab version of female.

Range & habitat Confined to extensive reedbeds, mostly in S and W Europe.

Nest Well-concealed cup in reeds.

Voice Listen for frequent characteristic *ping* calls. Rarely-heard song an undistinguished rattle.

General Erratic in occurrence and numbers, sensitive to severe weather, but locally fairly common.

MARSH TIT *Parus palustris*

Tiny (12 cm), black-capped tit, dull brown above, pale buffish below. Watch for neat appearance, small black bib. Best distinguished from Willow Tit (p.214) by call. Sexes similar.

Juvenile	Much as adult.
Range &	Year-round resident over much of central and W
habitat	Europe. Favours woodland, scrub and gardens.
Nest	Deserted tree hole.
Voice	Explosive *pit-choo* call; song a bell-like *pitchawee-oo*.
General	Widespread, but rarely numerous.

WILLOW TIT *Parus montanus*

Tiny (12 cm), black-capped tit, brownish above, pale buffish below. Watch for scruffy appearance, heavy head and neck, large dull cap and (sometimes) pale panel in wing. Best distinguished from Marsh Tit (p.213) by call. Sexes similar.

Juvenile Much as adult.

Range & Year-round resident over much of central, W and N
habitat Europe. Favours woodland, scrub and gardens.

Nest Excavates hole in rotten stump, hence thick neck muscles.

Voice Repetitive *dee*, *chay* or *eez* notes in call; song a musical warble.

General Widespread, but rarely numerous.

CRESTED TIT *Parus cristatus*

Tiny (12 cm) tit with distinctive black and white chequered crest. Body brown above, buff below; watch for white face and cheeks with black 'fish-hook' marking on cheek and black bib. Sexes similar.

Juvenile	As adult, but poorly marked with little crest.
Range & habitat	Year-round resident over much of Europe except extreme W and SE, in mature mixed or coniferous woodland. In Scotland confined to relict ancient pine forest.
Nest	Excavates tree hole.
Voice	Call characteristic purring *chirr*; song a high- pitched, repeated series of *tsee* notes.
General	Widespread; occasionally fairly common. Usually solitary or with other tits.

COAL TIT *Parus ater*

Tiny (12 cm) tit, active in canopy. Plump body olive or olive-grey above, pale buff below. Note white double wingbar. Watch for characteristic glossy black head with white cheeks and white patch on nape. Sexes similar.

Juvenile As adult, duller, with grey head markings.

Range & habitat Year-round resident, sometimes migrant, in European woodlands of all types, but favours mature conifers. Also gardens, parks, farmland, especially in winter.

Nest In hole or crevice in tree or bank.

Voice High-pitched *zeet* call; song a distinctive repeated series of *wheat-zee* phrases.

General Widespread, often common. Solitary or with other tits.

BLUE TIT *Parus caeruleus*

Tiny (12 cm), familiar tit, active in canopy. Back green, with cobalt-blue tail and dark blue wings with a single white wingbar. Underparts yellow. Watch for distinctive head pattern of pale blue crown, white eyestripe, black stripe through eye, white cheeks and black bib. Males usually brighter than females.

Juvenile Duller, greenish-grey instead of blue.

Range & habitat Year-round resident and migrant over much of Europe except far N. Seen almost anywhere except on mountains, moors and at sea.

Nest In hole or crevice in tree, bank or building.

Voice *See-see-see-sit* call; song an accelerating trill after *see-see-see* notes.

General Widespread, often common, frequently gregarious.

GREAT TIT *Parus major*

Small (15 cm); largest European tit, often terrestrial. Note olive back, bluish wings with white wingbar. Watch for glossy black head with white cheeks, relatively long robust beak. Black bib extends in line down middle of yellow underparts; darker and more extensive in male.

Juvenile	Duller, greenish-grey instead of black.
Range & habitat	Year-round resident or migrant over much of Europe, summer visitor to far N. Wide habitat, but favours woodlands, parks, gardens and farmland.
Nest	In hole or crevice in tree, bank or building.
Voice	Vocal, calls very varied: *chink* most common. Song also varied, characteristic *teacher-teacher* and *see-saw* phrases.
General	Widespread, often common.

NUTHATCH *Sitta europaea*

Small (15 cm), woodpecker-like. Moves head-up or head-down on branch (unlike woodpeckers). Watch for blue-grey back, white throat, black stripe through eye, longish dagger-like beak. Underparts buff, tinged deep chestnut on flanks of male. Tail short and square, white-tipped.

Juvenile As adult, but duller.

Range & habitat Year-round resident over much of Europe except far N and W. Favours deciduous woodland and parkland, occasionally gardens, especially in winter.

Nest In cavity, often in tree, usually with entrance hole plastered with mud to correct diameter.

Voice Distinctive ringing *chwit;* whistling *too-wee, too-wee* song.

General Widespread, locally fairly common.

TREECREEPER *Certhia familiaris*

Tiny (12 cm) mouse like, creeps up tree-trunks. Mottled brown back, white underparts. Watch for bold frowning eyestripe, downcurved beak, long stiff tail, buff wingbars distinctive in undulating flight. Sexes similar.

Juvenile	As adult, but more heavily buff-speckled.
Range & habitat	Resident in W, central, N and NE Europe; in mature woodland favouring conifers except in Britain and Ireland.
Nest	Usually in crevice behind flap of bark.
Voice	Sharp, shrill *zeee* call; song distinctive descending trill with final flourish.
General	Widespread, rarely numerous. Short-toed Treecreeper (*C. brachydactyla*): almost identical, widespread in central and S Europe. Favours deciduous woods. Subtly different *zeet* call.

GOLDEN ORIOLE *Oriolus oriolus*

Medium (25 cm) and starling-like. Male brilliant gold and black, with shortish pink beak. Female golden-olive above, whitish below with faint streaks: watch for yellow rump and yellow-tipped dark tail in flight.

Juvenile	As female, but duller, more olive.
Range & habitat	Summer visitor or migrant to much of Europe except N and far W. Favours mature open deciduous woodland and parkland, also orchards and groves.
Nest	Grassy hammock slung between twigs.
Voice	Very characteristic fluting *wheela-wee-oo* and *too-loo-ee* calls.
General	Widespread, not numerous, heard more than seen. Despite bright plumage, remarkably inconspicuous in canopy.

RED-BACK SHRIKE *Lanius collurio*

Small (18 cm) shrike. Watch for male's stubby hooked beak, rufous back, grey crown, black eyestripe and white-edged black tail. Female greyer and duller, scaly marks on breast, dark brown smudge through eye, tail brown.

Juvenile As female, duller and heavier marks on breast.

Range & habitat Summer visitor or migrant to much of Europe except far W. Favours dry open country with bushes, heath, scrub, also farmland.

Nest Neat grassy cup in bush.

Voice Harsh *chack* call; unexpected melodious warbling song.

General Widespread, rarely numerous. Woodchat Shrike (*L. senator*), summer visitor to S Europe: white underparts, black back, chestnut and black head, bold white wingbar.

GREAT GREY SHRIKE *Lanius excubitor*

Medium (25 cm); the largest shrike. Distinctively pale and long-tailed, uses prominent perches. Watch for hooked beak, black patch through eye, white on forehead and over eye. In deeply swooping flight shows grey rump, long white-edged black tail and broad white bars in black wings. Sexes similar.

Juvenile	Similar, but browner, barred on underparts.
Range & **habitat**	Year-round resident across central Europe, winter visitor to W and S, summer visitor to N. Favours open countryside with plentiful bushes, trees and scrub.
Nest	Grass cup in bush.
Voice	Harsh *chek* call; jangling song.
General	Widespread, never numerous.

JAY *Garrulus glandarius*

Medium (35 cm), colourful crow with distinctive pinkish-buff plumage. Watch for dark-flecked crown and black moustachial streaks. Flight looks floppy and hesitant on rounded wings: look for contrasting white rump and black tail, and for blue and white wing patches. Distinctive and unusual pale pink eye. Sexes similar.

Juvenile	As adult, but duller.
Range & habitat	Year-round resident over much of Europe except far N. Favours woodland, parks and farmland with plentiful mature trees.
Nest	Untidy twiggy shallow cup in tree fork.
Voice	Vocal; harsh *skaark* call; rarely heard soft chattering song.
General	Widespread, often fairly common.

NUTCRACKER *Nucifraga caryocatactes*

Medium (33 cm), dull-plumaged crow. Watch for straight, dark, dagger-like beak, brown cap, white-flecked body plumage. Bold white undertail coverts. In flight shows dark, rounded wings and white-tipped black tail. Sexes similar.

Juvenile	Similar to adult, but duller.
Range &	Year-round resident in conifer or mixed forests, often
habitat	mountainous, in N, central and E Europe. Occasionally occurs almost anywhere in W when food short.
Nest	Shallow twiggy cup in tree fork.
Voice	Vocal; harsh *skaark* and growling calls; jangling squeaky song.
General	Locally fairly common.

ALPINE CHOUGH *Pyrrhocorax graculus*

Medium (37 cm), slim, glossy-black crow. Watch for shortish, yellow, slightly downcurved beak, pink legs. Often aerobatic in flight, swooping and tumbling characteristically on rounded fingered wings. Sexes similar.

Juvenile Sooty, with grey legs and dull beak.
Range & habitat Resident at high altitudes in mountains of S Europe, often near cable-car stations.
Nest Twiggy platform in cave or crevice.
Voice Vocal; far-carrying *chee-up* or *skreee*.
General Locally fairly common. Red-billed Chough (*P. pyrrhocorax*): iridescent black with slim, downcurved crimson beak and red legs. At lower altitudes in S, on coastal cliffs in far W. *Kee-ow* call.

MAGPIE *Pica pica*

Medium (45 cm), unmistakable and familiar long-tailed pied crow. Watch for floppy flight on black and white rounded wings, long iridescent tapered tail cocked on landing. Often terrestrial. Sexes similar.

Juvenile	As adult, but duller, initially with shorter tail.
Range & habitat	Year-round resident over most of Europe. Wide habitat: woodland, farmland, scrub, parks and gardens.
Nest	Football-size dome of twigs, high in tree.
Voice	Harsh *chack* calls and chuckles; rarely heard quiet musical warbling song.
General	Widespread, locally common. Azure-winged Magpie (*Cyanopica cyanea*) of extreme SW Europe: pinkish-beige body, blue wings, long blue tail, black hood, whitish throat and collar.

JACKDAW *Corvus monedula*

Medium (33 cm) crow. Watch for stubby beak, black crown with slight crest, contrasting grey nape and striking white eye. In flight, has quicker wingbeats than other crows, wings rounded. Sexes similar.

Juvenile	As adult, but duller, lacking grey nape.
Range & habitat	Widespread resident except in N Europe. Wide habitat: woodland, farmland, city centres and coastal cliffs.
Nest	Usually in tree hole, rocky cleft or building.
Voice	Metallic *jack*, also high-pitched *keeaa*.
General	Widespread, often common, often gregarious. Occasionally sunbathes with seeming total relaxation, as do some other birds.

ROOK *Corvus frugilegus*

Medium (45 cm) crow. Watch for long, grey, dagger-like beak and bare white fleshy face contrasting with glossy iridescent black plumage. Loose feathers of upper leg give baggy-trousered appearance. Usually gregarious, often aerobatic, showing fingered wingtips. Sexes similar.

Juvenile	As adult, but duller, lacks face patch, has bristly base to straight-sided beak (see Carrion Crow, p.230).
Range & habitat	Year-round resident, sometimes migrant, over much of Europe, summer visitor in N, winter visitor to S. Favours farmland and open countryside with plentiful trees.
Nest	Colonial, bulky twig nest high in tree.
Voice	Vocal; raucous *kaar*.
General	Widespread, often common.

CARRION / HOODED CROW *Corvus corone*

Medium (45 cm) crow. All-black (Carrion) or grey with black head, wings and tail (Hooded) with intermediates where ranges overlap. Watch for black feathered base and curved ridge to beak, and neat, tight feathering to upper leg. Often solitary, in pairs or family groups, occasionally in flocks in winter. Sexes similar.

Juvenile	Much as adult, but duller.
Range &	Carrion: year-round resident in W and SW Europe;
habitat	Hooded: wider ranging through E and SE, central, N and NW, summer visitor to far N. Substantial overlap in central and S Europe. Favours all open countryside, also urban areas.
Nest	Solitary bulky twig structure high in tree.
Voice	Deep harsh *korr*.
General	Widespread.

RAVEN *Corvus corax*

Largest (63 cm) of the crows. Note thick neck, heavy head with bristling throat feathers, and massive angular beak. In flight, watch for broad heavily-fingered wings and distinctive wedge-shaped tail tip. Often solitary, in pairs or family groups. Sexes similar.

Juvenile	Similar to adult.
Range & habitat	Widespread year-round resident in coastal, moorland and mountain areas of W, S, E and N Europe, largely absent from central areas.
Nest	Very bulky twig structure in tree, or on rocky ledge.
Voice	Gruff *pruuk* and resonant *gronk*.
General	Though widespread, rarely numerous.

STARLING *Sturnus vulgaris*

Small (22 cm) and familiar. Watch for iridescent black plumage with buff speckling, denser in winter. Male sings from prominent perch, throat feathers bristling, wings flapping slowly. Beak yellow in summer, black in winter. Gregarious. Fast and direct flight on triangular wings. Sexes similar.

Juvenile Dull pale brown, darker above than below.

Range & habitat Year-round resident or migrant over much of Europe, summer visitor in N, winter visitor to SW. Occurs in almost all terrestrial habitats.

Nest Untidy straw and feathers in cavity.

Voice Vocal; harsh shrieking calls, song full of chattering notes and mimicry of other birds.

General Widespread and common.

HOUSE SPARROW *Passer domesticus*

Small (15 cm) and familiar. Watch for typical black triangular beak and head pattern of male, with grey crown, white cheeks, brown nape and black bib. Female pale fawn on underparts, mottled browns above; note pale eyestripe.

Juvenile Much as female.

Range & habitat Year-round resident throughout Europe except extreme N. Often near habitation, favours farmland and urban areas.

Nest Untidy spherical grassy structure in dense vegetation or hole.

Voice Harsh *chirrup,* often repetitive.

General Widespread, often common. Male Spanish Sparrow (*P. hispaniolensis*) from extreme S Europe: chestnut crown, white eyestripe, black-blotched breast; female indistinguishable from House Sparrow.

TREE SPARROW *Passer montanus*

Tiny (13 cm), but chunky, sparrow. Both sexes show head pattern of brown crown and narrow white collar. Watch for white cheeks with bold black spot and small black bib.

Juvenile As adult, but duller and browner.
Range & Resident, sometimes migrant, except in far N
habitat Europe. Favours woodland, farmland and scrub.
Nest Domed grass structure, often in cavity.
Voice Distinctively liquid *tek* and *tchup* calls.
General Widespread, sometimes fairly common. Drabber Rock Sparrow (*Petronia petronia*): sexes similar, resembles female House Sparrow. Has indistinct yellow spot on throat, distinctive white-tipped tail. Confined to rocky areas in extreme S.

CHAFFINCH *Fringilla coelebs*

Small (15 cm) finch. Pink breast, grey hood and black forehead in summer male, duller and masked by buff feather fringes in winter. Female olive-brown above, buff below. In flight, watch for white-edged blackish tail and bold, white, double wingbars in both sexes.

Juvenile Much as female.

Range & habitat Widespread year-round resident across Europe, summer visitor in N and E. Numbers in W and N augmented by migrants and winter visitors. Favours woodlands, farmland, parks and gardens. Often gregarious in winter.

Nest Neat, well-camouflaged cup in tree fork.

Voice Ringing *pink* call; song a powerful cascade of rich notes ending in a flourish.

General Widespread, often common.

BRAMBLING *Fringilla montifringilla*

Small (15 cm) finch. Glossy black head and back contrast with orange on breast and wings in summer male. At other times, black is partly concealed by broad orange-buff feather fringes. Female browner, but still orange on face and breast. In flight, watch for orange-white double wingbars and distinctive white rump.

Juvenile	Much as female.
Range & habitat	Summer visitor to N Europe, breeding in forest and woodland. Migrant or winter visitor to rest of Europe, favouring woodland, parks, gardens and farmland.
Nest	Neat, well-camouflaged cup in tree fork.
Voice	Drawn-out *chwaay* flight call; simple slow repetitive song based on *twee* notes.
General	Widespread, but erratic.

SERIN *Serinus serinus*

Tiny (10 cm) yellowish finch. Watch for streaked yellow-brown upperparts, bright yellow breast of male. Female duller and buffer. In flight, note yellow double wingbars and characteristic yellow rump contrasting with dark tail. Beak distinctively tiny and stubby, yet triangular.

Juvenile Much as female.

Range & habitat Summer visitor to W and central Europe, year-round resident further S. Favours open woodland, and farmland, parks and gardens with plenty of mature trees.

Nest Tiny neat moss and grass cup, usually high in tree.

Voice *Churr-lit* flight call and distinctive but monotonous jingling song.

General Widespread, locally fairly common.

FINCHES

GREENFINCH *Carduelis chloris*

Small (15 cm) yellowish finch with relatively heavy, pale triangular beak. Male olive-green above, rich yellow below. Shows yellow edge to folded wing, and grey shoulders. Female duller, buffish yellow on underparts with darker streaks. In flight, fanned, slightly forked tail shows yellow patches at either side of base.

Juvenile	Much as female.
Range & habitat	Year-round resident or migrant over much of Europe, summer visitor to far N. Favours scrub, open woodlands, parks, gardens and farmland.
Nest	Cup of twigs, moss and grass in tree or bush.
Voice	Drawn-out *dweeee* call; purring song in display flight with exaggerated wing beats.
General	Widespread, often common.

238

GOLDFINCH *Carduelis carduelis*

Tiny (13 cm) colourful finch. Watch for diagnostic red face, white cheeks, black crown and nape in adult. In flight, note forked tail, white rump, black wings with distinctively broad, full-length golden wingbar. Sexes similar.

Juvenile	Dull buff, lacking head pattern, but with white rump and broad gold wingbar.
Range & habitat	Year-round resident or migrant over much of Europe, summer visitor to parts of N and NE. Favours heath and scrub, but also open woodland, farmland, parks and gardens.
Nest	Neat, well-camouflaged hair and rootlet nest, usually high in canopy.
Voice	Sharp *dee-dee-lit* call; prolonged tinkling jingle of a song.
General	Widespread, often common.

SISKIN *Carduelis spinus*

Tiny (12 cm), dark, agile finch. Upperparts olive, tinged yellow and heavily dark streaked. Male has black cap and bib, yellow cheeks and upper breast; female lacks black, has paler streaked breast. In flight, watch for striking yellow wingbars, yellow rump and yellow patches at base of blackish forked tail.

Juvenile As adult female, but duller.

Range & habitat Year-round resident, migrant or winter visitor to much of Europe, summer visitor to far N. Breeds in woodlands and forest, in winter favours birch and alder, sometimes on farmland or in parks and gardens.

Nest Twiggy cup high in canopy, often in conifer.

Voice Flight call extended *chwee-ooo;* prolonged twittering song.

General Widespread, erratic, locally fairly common.

LINNET *Carduelis cannabina*

Tiny (13 cm), brownish finch. Male rich chestnut-brown on back, with white-edged dark tail, blackish wings with white panel. Watch for rich pink cap to buff head and pink breast, most conspicuous in summer. Winter male and female dull brown above, with paler streaked breast. Flight weakly fluttering, deeply undulating.

Juvenile	Much as female.
Range &	Year-round resident or migrant over much of Europe,
habitat	summer visitor in N. Favours heath, scrub and farmland, sometimes parks and gardens.
Nest	Neat, well-concealed grassy cup in shrub.
Voice	Loud *sweet* call; twittering song.
General	Widespread, locally common.

TWITE *Carduelis flavirostris*

Tiny (13 cm) finch, aptly called the mountain linnet.
Streaked dull brown above, buff with brown streaks below.
Triangular beak, grey in summer, yellow in winter. Watch
for single whitish wingbar and pink flush on breast and
rump of summer male, sexes otherwise similar.

Juvenile	Much as female.
Range & habitat	Year-round resident or winter visitor to NW coastal heath, hills and moorland, summer visitor further N. May winter on coastal marshes and rough grassland.
Nest	Well-concealed grassy cup low in shrub or on ground.
Voice	Nasal *chway* or *chweet;* musical jingling song.
General	Local, sometimes gregarious.

REDPOLL *Carduelis flammea*

Tiny (12 cm), compact, dark finch. Dark brown, heavily streaked above, paler buff below, streaked brown on breast. In summer, has dark red cap (poll), small black bib and male may have pink flush on breast. Note indistinct buff wingbar. Sexes similar in winter.

Juvenile As winter female, lacking bib.

Range & habitat Year-round resident, winter visitor or migrant to N, central and W Europe, summer visitor to far N. Favours mixed woodland, especially with birch, also scrub and open fields in winter in mixed flocks with other finches.

Nest Neat cup, usually high in tree.

Voice *Chee-chee-chit* call; purring trill of song as circles high over trees.

General Widespread, locally common, in places increasing.

CROSSBILL *Loxia curvirostra*

Small (15–17 cm), heavily-built finch with distinctively bulky, parrot-like crossed beak. Males orange-brown or crimson-brown, females greenish-olive. Note swooping flight showing notched tail and parrot-like acrobatics, feeding on conifer cones.

Juvenile Much as female.

Range & habitat Widespread year-round resident over much of Europe, irregular visitor elsewhere, sometimes staying to breed if food supplies allow. Favours conifers, particularly spruce.

Nest Flattish twiggy platform high in canopy.

Voice Metallic *jip* or *jup* call; abrupt twittering song.

General Widespread, erratic, locally fairly common.

BULLFINCH *Pyrrhula pyrrhula*

Small (15 cm), thick-set finch. Male has black cap, grey back and red underparts. Female has black cap, but is suede-brown above, pinkish-fawn below. Looks heavy-headed and slow in undulating flight. Watch for white rump and purplish-black tail.

Juvenile As female, but lacking black cap.

Range & habitat Widespread year-round resident, sometimes migrant, over much of Europe except far SW and SE. Favours woodlands with dense undergrowth, scrub, farmland with hedges, occasionally parks and gardens.

Nest Fragile shallow twiggy platform in shrub.

Voice Whistling *peeeuu*. Song a very quiet warble.

General Though widespread, rarely numerous. Usually solitary or in pairs.

HAWFINCH *Coccothraustes coccothraustes*

Small (18 cm), but one of the larger finches. Large chestnut head and huge, silvery, wedge-shaped beak with grey nape, brown back and pinkish-buff underparts. In deeply undulating flight watch for white-tipped tail and broad white wingbars. Sexes broadly similar.

Juvenile   Much as adult, but browner and duller.

Range &   Year-round resident or occasional migrant over
habitat   much of Europe except far N and NW. Favours
mature, usually deciduous, woodland with seeding
trees.

Nest   Bulky twiggy platform, high in canopy.

Voice   Explosive Robin-like *zik* call. Song a rarely-heard
twittering warble.

General   Widespread, rarely numerous. Secretive.

Snow Bunting *Plectrophenax nivalis*

Small (17 cm) bunting. Summer male unmistakably black and white. Female and winter male streaked brown above, paler and buffer below; black-tipped yellow beak. Always shows white in closed wing and conspicuous white mid-wing triangle and white sides to tail in flight.

Juvenile Similar to female.
Range & habitat Summer visitor breeding in far N Europe, migrant or winter visitor to NW and north-central areas. Breeds on tundra and mountainsides, winters on weedy fields and marshes.
Nest Grassy cup, concealed in rocky crevice.
Voice Plaintive *sweet* and *tew* calls; fast-moving Skylark-like song.
General Irregular, rarely numerous.

YELLOWHAMMER *Emberiza citrinella*

Small (18 cm), familiar yellowish bunting. Summer male brilliantly yellow-breasted, with yellow head showing few darker markings. Female and winter male duller and browner, but still with yellow on head and underparts. Note dark-streaked rich chestnut mantle and rump.

Juvenile	Similar to female, but duller.
Range & habitat	Widespread year-round resident over much of Europe, summer visitor in far N, winter visitor in extreme S. Favours heath, scrub, farmland and grassland with bushes.
Nest	Grassy cup low in shrub.
Voice	Abrupt *twick* call; familiar song, a rattle of *zit* notes ending in a drawn-out wheezing *tzeeee*.
General	Widespread, often fairly common.

CIRL BUNTING *Emberiza cirlus*

Small (16 cm) southern bunting. Male has grey-green hood with black and yellow markings, dark-streaked chestnut back, chestnut flanks and yellow belly. Female and winter male duller and browner, similar to female Yellowhammer (p.248). All show distinctive olive rump in flight.

Juvenile	Similar to female.
Range & habitat	Resident in W, SW and S Europe. Favours dry heath and scrub.
Nest	Grassy cup concealed low in shrub.
Voice	High-pitched soft *tsip* call; song a monotonous rattle of *zit* notes, lacking final *tzeee* of Yellowhammer.
General	Locally fairly common. Uses prominent bush-top song-posts.

ORTOLAN *Emberiza hortulana*

Small (15 cm), drab bunting. Summer male has grey hood and breast, with yellow throat and eye-ring, dull chestnut underparts. Female and winter male duller, streaked dull brown above, with buff throat and cinnamon breast. Watch for distinctive pale eye-ring and pale pinkish beak. Shows white-edged tail in flight.

Juvenile	Similar to female, but more uniformly buff.
Range & habitat	Summer visitor or migrant over much of Europe, scarcer in W and N. Favours dry open country and farmland with scattered scrub, often on hillsides.
Nest	Well-concealed grassy cup.
Voice	*Pwit*, *tlip* and *chew* flight calls; slow rasping song of several *zeeu* notes.
General	Though widespread, rarely numerous.

REED BUNTING *Emberiza schoeniclus*

Small (15 cm) bunting. Summer male has striking black
and white head pattern. Female and winter male browner,
streaked; dark head with pale eyestripe, and blackish
moustachial streaks. Tail black, white-edged.

Juvenile Similar to female.

Range & habitat Resident over much of Europe. Usually in marshy
areas, occasionally elsewhere.

Nest Grassy cup concealed low in vegetation.

Voice *Seep* and measured *see-you* calls; song a short,
harsh and disjointed jangle.

General Widespread, locally common. Scarce Lapland
Bunting (*Calcarius lapponicus*): chestnut nape, pale
crown stripe, *ticky-tick-teeu* call; winters on coastal
marshes.

CORN BUNTING *Miliaria calandra*

Small (18 cm), but the largest bunting, and also the least distinctive in plumage. Upperparts brown, heavily darker streaked, underparts pale buff with brown streaking. Note thick-set appearance, bulky stubby beak. Shows no white in wings or tail in flight. Sexes similar, winter and summer.

Juvenile	Similar to adult.
Range & habitat	Erratically distributed across much of Europe except N. Favours open, dryish farmland, heath and grassland.
Nest	Well-concealed grassy cup on ground.
Voice	*Tsip* or *quit* call; song unmistakable grating metallic harsh jangle, from prominent perch.
General	Though widespread, numbers very variable.

Index

COLLINS GEM
BABIES' names

COLLINS GEM
BEER

COLLINS GEM
BIRDS

COLLINS GEM
CALORIE Counter

COLLINS GEM
FACT FILE

COLLINS GEM
FENG SHUI

COLLINS GEM
FLAGS

COLLINS GEM
Healthy EATING

COLLINS GEM
QUOTATIONS

COLLINS GEM
SAS Self-Defence

COLLINS GEM
SAS Survival Guide

COLLINS GEM
SEASHORE

COLLINS GEM
TREES

COLLINS GEM
Understanding DREAMS

COLLINS GEM
WILD flowers

COLLINS GEM
WINE Dictionary